Glimpses of Grace

WALKING IN HOPE THROUGH ALZHEIMER'S AND ORDINARY DAYS

Dorothy Horne

ISBN: 1503149781
ISBN 13: 9781503149786

Contact information:

https://www.dorothyhorneauthor.com
www.news-journal.com - "Glimpses of Grace"
dothorne@yahoo.com
P.O. Box 5811; Longview, TX 75608-5811

Cover design by Bettye Craddock
Cover photograph by Karly Brooks
Library of Congress Control Number: 2015903847
CreateSpace Independent Publishing Platform
North Charleston, South Carolina

To my family,
who allowed me to share our story
as we walk in hope

To all people and families
living with Alzheimer's disease

STANDING: MARK, AMANDA, BYRON, DOROTHY, KARLY AND TREY
SITTING: CASE—2, KARL—4, NATHANIEL—7 AND CANNON—2

Acknowledgments

So many wonderful people have helped or encouraged me in some way during the process of assimilating these columns into a book. I found it does indeed "take a village" (or in my case, several towns). God provided caring people to help each step of the way, and I am grateful to the following individuals who helped make this book possible:

—*Richard Brack*, editor, Longview News-Journal, for his generous endorsement of the book as well as his encouragement and guidance. I am grateful for his admonition several years ago to "keep writing" and the opportunities he has given me to have a voice.

—*Juan Elizondo*, managing editor of the Longview News-Journal (2006-10), for his kind endorsement and advice, and for turning me into an "accidental columnist" five years ago.

—*Gary Borders*, East Texas newspaper man and columnist, for his gracious endorsement and for generously offering his time and expertise to edit the columns at the beginning of this venture. I owe much to his guidance and encouragement.

—*Paul Anderson*, who helped me with all the technical aspects of compiling the manuscript, and also served as referee between me and my computer. His invaluable assistance and advice were instrumental in bringing this book to fruition and I am deeply grateful.

—*Bettye Craddock*, who graciously offered her time and expertise to design the cover, provide technical advice and edit the final additions to the manuscript. I am beholden to her, and could not have finished the book without her support and assistance.

—*Jo Lee Ferguson*, who volunteered her expertise to edit the final book proof. I am grateful to her for her suggestions, support and marketing help.

—*Mac McCoy*, my awesome geek brother, for creating my website and tutoring me in all things technical.

—*Susan Foster*, my dear friend who has supported me and prayed for this project from the very beginning.

—*Our daughters and sons-in-law: Amanda, Karly, Mark and Trey,* for their support and unconditional love; and *our precious grandsons: Nathaniel, Karl, Cannon and Case.* The love, joy and laughter they bring us are precious jewels.

—*Byron*, the love of my life, my inspiration and my rock. He has blessed me beyond measure by loving me and modeling how to live and thank God in all circumstances. I am indebted to him for his help and support while I worked on the manuscript and also for his feedback and contributions to the columns. Together we will continue to walk in hope.

I am also grateful to the following people who have supported me and helped in various ways: *Scott Brunner, Sonya Reeder, Vickie Phelps, East Texas Christian Writing group, Roxie's Reading group, "Unforgettable Tuesdays" volunteers, our church family and friends and all the kind people along the way who encouraged me or told me they were inspired by a column.* I am humbled and blessed to be surrounded by your love and support.

To God be the glory

A Few Notes

Glimpses of Grace: Walking in Hope Through Alzheimer's and Ordinary Days, includes essays, stories and poems published in the Longview News-Journal print edition or the Longview News-Journal online blog, *"Glimpses of Grace"* from 2009–2014.

The **Alzheimer's Association** is the world's leading health organization in Alzheimer's care, support and research. Its mission is to eliminate the disease through the advancement of research; to provide and enhance care and support for all affected; and to reduce the risk of dementia through the promotion of brain health. Find out more information about Alzheimer's, clinical drug trials, speak to their Helpline or find a chapter or support group at www.alz.org.

You might notice that in almost every column pertaining to mental illness, I mention **NAMI** (National Alliance on Mental Illness). NAMI was a lifesaver for our family and offers invaluable resources for anyone dealing with mental illness. It is the nation's largest grassroots mental health organization and advocates for access to services, treatment, support and research. Find out more and locate a chapter or support group at www.nami.org.

You might also notice I frequently quote author and theologian **Frederick Buechner.** I have read and reread his books over the years and his writings on faith and life have left an indelible impression on me. He taught me to, "Listen to your life…in the last analysis, all moments are key moments, and life itself is grace."

Table of Contents

Preface

THE ACCIDENTAL COLUMNIST

I wrote my first "column" by accident when the Longview News-Journal's managing editor asked if he could run my "Letter to the Editor" about mental illness on the Saturday Forum page instead.

It was the summer of 2009. Our daughter had been diagnosed two years prior with severe postpartum depression and obsessive-compulsive disorder (OCD) after the birth of her first son. We had been trying to navigate the maze of the mental health system since the onset of her illness, and continually came across ignorance and stigma surrounding mental illness. I felt a need to give voice about all we had been witnessing.

Our daughter courageously gave me permission to share our family's experience, "because if it helps someone else not to feel alone, then it's worth it," she said.

After that first column, I continued submitting to the Forum page on a regular basis because it was such a wonderful way to help educate and raise awareness about mental illness. There was also another reason—I wanted to share the serendipitous "glimpses of grace" and God's provision we had been blessed with along the way. I never would have guessed the heartbreak of mental illness could also include so many blessings, but that is God's way.

Thanks be to Him, our daughter is in now in recovery.[1] She remains a staunch supporter and advocate for those struggling with the disease.

---

1 *Recovery* is a process, beginning with diagnosis and eventually moving into success-ful management of your illness. Successful recovery involves learning about your ill-ness and the treatments available, empowering yourself through the support of peers and family members, and finally moving to a point where you take action to manage your own illness by helping others. *(Source: nami.org)*

In November of 2011 my husband was diagnosed with early onset Alzheimer's. *At least,* we said to ourselves, *we already know God will provide and that there will be blessings in this journey, too.* So I continued to write, and prayed that I would remain open to sensing His presence and seeing through eyes of faith.

Many of the essays in this book chronicle how living with Alzheimer's has affected our lives, our family and our faith as we continue to walk this road. There are a variety of other stories, reflections and humorous observations, also. Our road weaves through light and laughter and alongside the quiet grace of ordinary days.

In these writings I choose to acknowledge but not focus on the negative aspects of living with the disease, but rather on how God is working through it as our family seeks to walk with His provision and strength. His grace is the golden thread that binds us together. Glimpses of this grace, like shooting stars, have consistently penetrated our darkness and illuminated a basic truth: *all* is grace.

Therefore, the overlying theme of the book is not about a disease but rather about God's grace, hope and provision in all circumstances. The purpose of the book is to point towards God as the source of strength and light. I pray it will serve as a vehicle for giving Him the glory.

I will praise you, O Lord, with all my heart;
I will tell of all Your wonders. I will be glad and rejoice in You;
I will sing praise to Your name, O Most High.

—Psalm 9:1, 2 (NIV)

Introduction

*M*any people have asked us about the process that led to Byron's diagnosis. Usually it is because they have concerns about a family member and are not sure about the right time to seek medical advice. Or perhaps they have already done so and the primary care doctor has dismissed their concerns. (Some primary care physicians do not take seriously enough the early signs of memory loss, which may or may not indicate the onset of Alzheimer's.)

Byron was admitted to his second drug trial six months ago to test the drug, Solanezubam (Eli Lilly & Co.), which targets beta amyloid, a toxic protein which builds up in the brains of individuals with Alzheimer's. (He also participated in a drug trial last year for five months before it was halted for failing to reach its goals.)

Whether or not this current drug benefits Byron, he is still, by his involvement, helping advance the research for a cure. For him, that is sufficient reason to participate because there are more than 5 million Americans currently living with Alzheimer's, at a cost to the nation of $214 billion.

Our story began about five or six years ago when I began to notice slight changes in Byron's memory. (Our family was unable to tell the difference—this is common.) His memory had always been superb. In fact, I had always counted on his memory because it was so much easier for me to use than sticky notes. Even with a loss, it was still better than mine.

When it came time for his yearly physical examination, I asked him to mention my concerns to his doctor to see if he had any suggestions. (I don't know why I thought that would work.) When Byron got home from his appointment, I asked what the doctor said. "He asked me if I had any concerns about my memory, and I told him no," Byron said. Apparently that was good enough for the doctor. (This kind of thing happens quite frequently, from what others have told me about their experiences.)

The next year when it was time for his physical, I went to his appointment with him. This did not go over well with Byron. I told the doctor my concerns, and he sent me back to the waiting room while he gave Byron a short memory test. About 10 minutes later, he called me back in and told me Byron had passed with flying colors and was *perfectly fine.*

Then I made them both mad. "I know you don't think there is anything wrong," I told the doctor, "but I live with him and I know there are changes. Would you please refer him to a neurologist anyway?" He grudgingly agreed to do so.

We made the appointment, and the neurologist gave Byron a more extensive memory test. He had concerns and referred Byron to a neuropsychologist, who administered a full-day battery of tests that covered the gamut: attention and memory, reasoning and problem-solving, visual-spatial function, language functions, sensory-perceptual functions, motor functions, academic skills, and emotional functioning.

Byron tested "normal" or "superior" in all areas except for a "severe deficit" in short-term memory. His official diagnosis was "mild cognitive impairment." We were told this condition could eventually lead to Alzheimer's, but not necessarily. Byron was prescribed two memory medications (Namenda and Razydyne) which research has shown helps slow down memory loss for a period of time.

On a beautiful fall gem of a day about a year later the neurologist first dropped the "A" word. I was hiking up a hill beside the Paul Boorman trail and my cell phone rang. I did not want to answer it because I knew who it was.

I had left Byron's neurologist a message earlier in the day about recent changes I had noticed in Byron's memory. As I stood there on the trail the doctor told me that it sounded like Byron was entering the early stages of Alzheimer's. To confirm his suspicions he wanted to schedule a spinal tap to check for biomarkers in the spinal fluid, which indicate the disease. I remember feeling numb and realizing that our lives had just changed.

The results came back positive, and on November 9, 2011, Byron was officially diagnosed with early onset Alzheimer's disease at age 62.

We were both devastated and understandably, Byron did not want anyone to know. About a week later, I met a man at an Alzheimer's support group who had also been diagnosed with early onset Alzheimer's several months prior. He seemed accepting and upbeat about his diagnosis so I asked him if he would be willing to reach out to Byron.

The next day he gave Byron a call and strongly encouraged him against keeping the disease a secret. His words helped give Byron the courage to step forward and unashamedly acknowledge his disease.

After that, the next thing Byron did was go on living his life the way he always had—with humor and *joie de vivre.*

He has walked this road for three years now and I have seen many people touched by his courage, acceptance and faith. We trust that what we are going through is not in vain, and that God will continue to use Byron and his situation for His purposes.

Even though we do not understand the big picture, we know there is one.

November 2014

Help Build Bridges

FOR THOSE WITH MENTAL ILLNESS

(Original "Letter-to-the-Editor-turned-column")

I would like to thank the Longview News-Journal staff for their continued coverage of mental illness, homelessness, and other related issues. The stigma and ignorance surrounding these societal problems are so great that it will take much continued coverage and education of the public before understanding, acceptance and change can take place. I applaud the News-Journal for frequently putting these issues before the public. Otherwise, out of sight, out of mind, and things will continue as they have been. That is unacceptable.

What we can do as a community is to become educated about mental illness and reach out to those people who need help and advocate for them, because until they come to a stable, balanced place in their minds, they will remain voiceless. We must care and be compassionate enough to stand in the breach for them in the meantime.

Until the stigma is reduced, the risks of being ostracized are too great for all but the bravest to speak up. I dream of a world in which mental illness—a brain disorder, a physical illness of the mind and not a character flaw—is accepted and treated like any other physical illness without stigma, disdain or pity.

Those who deal first-handedly with mental illness are my heroes. I don't think most people realize how determined, steadfast and brave they must be hour after hour and day after day to take the steps needed for recovery, such as finding the correct medications and proper therapy that will help release their minds from the captivity of the illness.

Unfortunately, many are ashamed to admit they are suffering from a mental illness for fear of being stigmatized, so they suffer in silence. Family members also suffer, often feeling unable to ask for prayers or support as one would be able to do for a diagnosis such as heart disease, cancer or diabetes.

And what about the people who don't have the family support, knowledge, economic means or resources to help them through their illness? For many there is no help and no place to go. They may self-medicate with drugs or alcohol and fall through the cracks and into our streets and prisons.

People with mental illness need family support and community support. They need compassion, not ridicule and condemnation. They need affordable medications and treatment. They need to have the opportunity to regain their lives and be productive members of society.

We need to advocate for people with mental illness. We need to contact our representatives and tell them not to cut funds for mental health services.

We need to knock down the walls of stigma and instead build bridges of support, understanding and acceptance.

To journey for the sake of saving our own lives is little by little to cease to live in any sense that really matters, even to ourselves, because it is only by journeying for the world's sake—even when the world bores and sickens and scares you half to death—that little by little we start to come alive...by grace I glimpsed that road and saw that it is the only one worth traveling.

—Frederick Buechner (*The Sacred Journey*)

July 11, 2009

Out of the Darkness

A FAMILY'S JOURNEY

Sometimes the landscape of our lives suddenly changes. You wake up one day in an unrecognizable place and realize you have no road map, no familiar landmarks, and worse, no directions to get back home.

In our case, the new landscape was mental illness. Our daughter was diagnosed with severe postpartum depression after the birth of our first grandchild.

Severe depression is one of a number of illnesses such as bipolar disorder, panic disorder, obsessive-compulsive disorder, and schizophrenia that are considered mental illnesses. According to statistics, one in four people have some type of mental illness, be it mild or severe.

Mental illness stems from a brain disorder which can be triggered by many factors such as hormonal imbalance, chemical imbalance, stress or a traumatic event. Severe mental illness is a devastating and life-changing occurrence, but it generally goes unacknowledged because mental illness is the elephant in the room.

After the onset of our daughter's illness, we felt helpless and overwhelmed. We needed medical help, information and advice and we needed it right then. But what we found was that to navigate the maze of the mental healthcare system, you need to get in line and wait your turn, which could take weeks, months, or years. Make as many phone calls as you like—it makes no difference.

Five months later we were still trying to navigate through the maze when I came across our first ray of hope—an announcement in the Longview News-Journal.

It said that the National Alliance on Mental Illness was going to sponsor a Family-to-Family course, 12-week educational classes for family members and caregivers of people with mental illness. The curriculum would focus on the clinical treatment of major psychiatric illnesses. It would also provide knowledge and skills that families need when faced with the difficulties of mental illness.

I had never heard of NAMI, even after all those months of phone calls and research; it sounded like an answer to our prayers. There were 20 spots available and I couldn't get to the phone fast enough. Maybe we would finally find some answers and other families who were going through similar experiences.

When the day finally arrived for the first class, I was nervous and wondered if we would recognize anyone. I kind of hoped that we wouldn't. The stigma, you know. I wondered what kind of people we would encounter in this "behind the scenes" world of mental illness.

We soon found out—all kinds, and from all walks of life. Mental illness does not respect of race, religion, or socio-economic status. We all had a common denominator—a family member with a mental illness.

Two trained NAMI facilitators, who also had family members with mental illness, put us at ease. There were lots of tears that night as we all shared our pain and helplessness. But there was also immense relief and comfort knowing that finally, there was a place we could share our struggles and have people understand. The class members all agreed that the NAMI classes were life preservers thrown to us.

During the first class session we learned about the cycle of grief one goes through when a family member is diagnosed with mental illness. We were not surprised to learn that it is like experiencing a death in the family. We learned about coping, and how to let go and better empathize with what our family member suffers. We gained respect for our family member's courage and begin to accept the things we could not change. We encouraged, cried, laughed and were there for each other. Through the NAMI classes, we were able to begin to let go and progress through pain and grief to acceptance and finally, to focus our energy on educating the public, confronting the system, and fighting the discrimination and stigma. It is only then we can truly make a difference for our loved ones.

January 10, 2011

Mental Illness and Catch-22

The doctor said it was supposed to be good—this new short-term acute care hospital. Now it had our daughter in it for severe postpartum depression. Since she had needed help immediately, we had to take his word for it. There was no time not to.

We didn't call it mental illness yet, because we weren't really sure what that was. We didn't call it anything, even to ourselves, for a long time. I guess we thought that would make it less real, like a bad dream, and we would wake up and go back to our normal lives.

My husband, son-in-law and I, along with our 2-week-old grandson, were in the hospital lobby, waiting for visiting hour to begin. It was our first time. Our daughter had been admitted only the day before, but it already seemed like a lifetime ago. We tried to make small talk, but doing "small" is hard when the pain is so large.

"You may come up now," said a pleasant young man. He smiled as he held the elevator door open for us. The simple kindness of strangers—it helps, sometimes.

When we stepped out of the elevator, our grandson began to cry. His daddy tried to calm him. None of us knew what to expect, or do.

The young man then escorted us to a large, nondescript room partitioned into cubicles. We were barely acknowledged by the nurse at the front desk when we asked where we might find our daughter. She pointed towards the back and after weaving our way through the cubicles we finally located her—propped up in a chair, head down and eyes half-closed.

"Hello, sweetie." We tried to rouse her. "Look who came to see you." Her eyes struggled to open as she attempted to focus. Then she saw her newborn son. Still trying to keep her eyes open, she managed a smile, wobbly held out her arms and leaned forward to kiss him. Before she made it to his cheek, however, her head dropped down again and she nodded off.

That is when I finally broke down.

Her 2-week-old son never received his mommy's kiss. That moment haunts me even now when I think about it.

I hurried back to the nurse at the front desk. "I think my daughter is over-medicated," I said. "Can you please tell the doctor?"

"I'm sorry, ma'am," she replied, not bothering to hide her annoyance. "She is an adult and she will have to tell the doctor herself."

I was stunned and suggested to the nurse just how impossible that would be. She shrugged. "That's the rule," she said, and went back to her paperwork.

So my daughter was too drugged to tell the doctor she was too drugged...I believe you would call that a *Catch-22*: *A situation in which a desired outcome or solution is impossible to attain because of a set of inherently illogical rules or conditions.*

That's it all right.

Thus began our initiation into the seemingly alternate universe of the mental health system.

Like rats in a maze of misinformation and red tape, we hit walls every which way we turned. Not surprisingly, one of the things we did find out is that Texas ranks 50th among the states for mental health resources.

Then one day a small, mustard seed-sized tidbit of information that I almost didn't even notice led us to a real live doorway—the National Alliance on Mental Illness (NAMI).

We learned that NAMI helps fill the gap between scarce mental health resources and individuals and families who need them. Through the classes we gained not only knowledge and understanding about mental illnesses, treatments and available options, but perhaps most importantly, we gained a community. We finally did not have to go it alone. Yes, I think that was the best part.

March 24, 2012

Broken

CAMP GILMONT

I don't like broken. I don't like my plans broken and I don't like my circumstances broken.

And I really don't like the people I love broken.

The Bible says that broken is good. In fact, it sounds like everything that is good comes out of brokenness. Why did God set it up like that?

Four years ago our daughter was diagnosed with a severe mental illness after the birth of our first grandchild. None of us knew anything about mental illness and had no idea of what to do or where to go for help. We were terrified.

She was admitted to a short-term psychiatric facility in order to get started on medication and stabilized. I cried and prayed and begged God to deliver our daughter from the crippling prison of her mind. I didn't know how to get her back. Having to stand by helplessly while my child suffered was the worst thing I had ever endured. When I couldn't see God working, I got angry.

However, I was her mother and had always been able to take care of her, so I decided to take charge, because that's what mothers do. I began an all-consuming search for information, assistance, answers and cures. I scoured the Internet, read books, and talked to agencies and health care professionals. What I found was lots of red tape, little information, few choices, long waiting lists and no answers.

At the end of my own resources and sufficiency, I had to admit that I was powerless to save my daughter—the circumstances were out of my control. I had no choice but to give her to God. For the first time the Genesis story about Abraham and his son, Isaac, made sense to me. God asked Abraham to offer Isaac to Him, and Abraham was willing even though he thought the outcome would be death. He trusted that somehow, God would provide. And God did. I asked Him to grant me that same trust.

In His own time, God blessed our daughter with recovery through a combination of medication, therapy, family support, and a steadfast spirit.

She and her husband now have two beautiful little boys. Although she will always have her illness, her symptoms are now minimal. She is able to manage them through medication and healthy lifestyle choices, just as others do with medical conditions such as heart disease or diabetes.

It was a long, painful journey, but also one filled with grace and mercy. All along the way God worked through brokenness. He brought our family closer together. He gave our daughter the strength to share her story so others suffering with mental illness would have hope and know they are not alone.

When Jesus said, "Blessed are the poor in spirit, for theirs is the kingdom of heaven," perhaps it is because only when we are broken can He can begin to accomplish His will in our lives.

Brokenness offers two paths. One path is fear, bitterness and despair. It begins in darkness and ends in darkness. The other path—faith, trust and hope. It begins in darkness but ends in light. Jesus is that path, because He was broken, too—for us. His path leads to the Kingdom.

I still don't like broken, but I do not fear it like I used to. Even when I can't see the light, I can still feel the path.

Sometimes the biggest miracles God performs are not in our circumstances but in our hearts.

My grace is sufficient for you, for my power is made perfect in weakness.

—2 Corinthians 12:9 (NIV)

November 22, 2011

Shattering the Stereotypes

OF MENTAL ILLNESS

*J*ason Green was a big man, a football player at one time, with a beautiful smile. When I first met him, I got the feeling that he was a person who genuinely cared about people. Jason was for real.

I could tell he was an analytical thinker—soft-spoken and to the point with a quiet intensity, his faith casually integrated into his conversation.

What I couldn't tell was that Jason had schizophrenia. It was triggered while he was in college. Schizophrenia, like other mental illnesses, is a brain disorder that usually is dormant until early adulthood, then emerges to interrupt the lives of young people in their prime. Jason did nothing to deserve it. He wasn't a bad person, just one who had the misfortune to be struck by a mental illness.

After his illness surfaced, Jason was in denial and refused treatment, not wanting the stigma of a mental illness label. He thought he could handle it himself. His family begged and pleaded with him to get help, but the law says that if the ill family member is an adult, nothing can be legally done until the person harms either himself or someone else. Usually that is too late, because by then the person has ended up in the prison system or the grave.

For Jason, the next ten years were hell—drug and alcohol addiction, jail stints, and at times—living on the streets. But Jason was one of the lucky ones. His family never gave up on him and they were finally able to convince him to get treatment. He still had a hard road ahead, because the longer mental illness goes untreated, the more difficult it is to reach a point of recovery.

However, Jason made it. He credited his recovery to God, his family, medication, and not giving up.

I met him when he gave a talk to our NAMI "Family-to-Family" class. His story broke my stereotypical thinking about mental illness.

In addition to giving talks to different groups about his illness, Jason held down a full-time job and facilitated a NAMI "Peer-to-Peer" group (educational classes for people with mental illnesses). Although he was in recovery, he acknowledged that he would always have schizophrenia. He still heard voices in his head, but he had learned how to distract himself so they weren't as noticeable to him. He wore earphones and listened to music, or interacted with people and involved himself in activities. He knew that in recovery it was important to take care of himself by eating right, getting enough sleep, exercising, avoiding "triggers," and taking his medication.

Jason was a special person—an inspiration to all. His mission was to advocate for people who have mental illnesses so that our community can become more educated about these devastating brain disorders. They deserve our admiration and prayers for the courage they display while facing their illness—not disdain, ridicule, or stigmatization.

It is a mission we all need to undertake.

June 13, 2009

The Wall

The difference is a wall. We have one, they don't. Upon it we hang not only our hats and diplomas, but also our judgments and our prejudices.

The wall serves to block our view. We can't see their faces; therefore we can pretend they are not there. I'm not proud of this, but sometimes when I encountered them on the street, I used to turn my face away. I'm not sure why—feared maybe, or so I wouldn't have to acknowledge their need or pain.

That all changed for me three years ago.

"Tell her to hang in there and not give up."

"Tell her we'll be praying for her."

"Tell her we know she will make it."

"Come back and tell us how she's doing."

These comments were made not at the gym, or church or work, but at a transitional living facility for the homeless in Longview called Fredonia Place.

The residents at the facility were diagnosed with mental illnesses and many also had substance abuse problems. As part of their treatment they were all participating in a "Peer-to-Peer" Education Program—"Recovery: Learning to Live Well," a nine-week course sponsored by NAMI.

My husband and I were representing the NAMI "Family-to-Family" classes (for family members of individuals diagnosed with a mental illness). We were there to share our story with the residents so they could get a perspective from a family member's experience of dealing with the mental illness of a loved one. We told them about our daughter and how she had been diagnosed with severe postpartum depression and obsessive-compulsive disorder after the birth of her baby.

I honestly did not expect the residents to be particularly interested in hearing our story; I went to Fredonia House a bit wary and with preconceived notions.

But how very wrong I was. They listened with empathy and understanding and offered to pray for her. We were humbled and grateful; those residents became Christ's hands and feet to us.

After our talk we mingled with the residents and listened to their stories and dreams. They were just broken people looking for what they had lost, not so different from you and me—except they did not turn their faces away.

At Fredonia Place a miracle happened for us. Where there had been a wall, our homeless friends had created a door. As we left, I turned to Byron and asked, "What just happened?"

Then the realization dawned on us—we had been standing on Holy Ground.

September 5, 2009

Love it Quick

YOU AIN'T GONNA HAVE IT LONG

"*L*ove it quick, you ain't gonna have it long." It sounded "deep," and I liked it. My sociology professor said that's all we needed to know, and I believed him. I stored it away in my memory to pull out later, because then there was lots of time left. After all, I was 18, and the world stretched before me like a smooth paved road. I expected that by the time I graduated, I would have my diploma in one hand, and "The Answers" in the other.

What I found when I set out, though, was that the smooth road turned out to be an alluring illusion. Twists, turns, bumps and ruts were the norm. Sometimes I was jolted off the road, other times I simply left it, later wondering if I'd ever find my way back again. I passed many people, places and moments along that road that I didn't love quickly. I had forgotten I wasn't going to have them long.

I missed opportunities to appreciate, accept and forgive. It's the human condition—"don't know what you got 'til it's gone." We are all fellow travelers on that same road. Friends disappoint, the child is lost, the job disappears, the marriage ends, health fails, dreams die, hearts harden, and death claims. And the refrain plays on, "Love it quick, you ain't gonna have it long."

And then I discovered that my professor had been only half right. His assumptions, passed along to naïve college freshmen, had been based on "chronos" time, earthly time, which has a beginning and an end. That's where the "ain't gonna have it long" part fits in. But what I didn't know about was "kairos" time, God's time. It cannot be measured, and encompasses not only the past and present, but also the future.

In God's time, what seems to be an ending also contains the seeds of a beginning—the promise of a "Second Half." God's purpose will continue in these unmeasured moments of time, both on earth and in heaven—in other words, in eternity. God is the God of "long enough." He is our strength and our portion.

In God's time, all will be made right, and all will be made new. The story will go on. "What's lost is nothing to what's found and all the death that ever was, set next to life, would scarcely fill a cup" (Frederick Buechner, *Listening to Your Life*).

No, life does not usually turn out the way we thought it would, but is redeemed according to God's purposes. He doesn't give us all the answers, and wants us to trust him with the questions. "*Love it quick, you ain't gonna have it long.*"

But it will be long enough. God's time, not ours.

January 30, 2010

Planting Alleluias

*C*hildren are natural miracle-finders and joy-gatherers. Like curious squirrels, they scamper from branch to branch and tree to tree—seeking, exploring and discovering. Buoyed by the love and support of the ones who celebrate them, they rarely fall. I learned that from 20 years of teaching first and second graders. Provide a nourishing environment, and they will flourish.

Children go to bed each night with miracles under their pillows and joy in their hearts. That is the way it is supposed to be.

But, there are no guarantees on "supposed to be." For the less fortunate and uncelebrated children who have little scaffolding, the world is not a predictable or safe place.

Their miracles lie withered and dusty on the bedroom floor, and hope is only a faint light under a closed door.

A little girl in my class, Sheila (not her real name), was one of those children. She had no solid ground under her and possessed a gifted mind but a spiritless, sad countenance.

There were no miracles under Sheila's pillow at night.

She stole from her classmates—crayons, erasers, money, anything. It did not matter to her; neither did consequences or lack of friends. The children did not want to be around her. I was frustrated with my inability to find a way to stop her self-defeating behaviors.

At age 8, she was already losing her way, and something had to change.

Sheila needed a miracle.

I came across a poem titled "Greenless Child," by Ann Weems. It ends with these lines:

Oh, who will touch this greenless child? Who will plant alleluias in her heart and send her dancing into all the colors of God? Or will she be left like an unwrapped package on the kitchen table, too dull for anyone to take the trouble. Does God think we're her keeper?

As I read the poem, I realized it contained the seeds of Sheila's miracle. Our class would be her "keeper" and *we* would "plant alleluias in her heart."

While Sheila was out of the room the next day for a special class, I talked with my students about how she needed our acceptance and love, no matter what she did. I asked them if they would be willing to forgive Sheila for stealing from them. No one is more compassionate, loving and forgiving than a child, so it was no surprise when they said yes. (No wonder Jesus said, "Become like little children.")

For the next hour the class wrote letters to Sheila. They told her they forgave her for stealing and would always love her, no matter what she did. They meant it. I knew it, and the next day after Sheila read each one of their letters aloud, she knew it, too. She cried and we cried, but they were all tears of joy.

Alleluias were planted in Sheila's heart, and for perhaps the first time, she went to bed that night with miracles under her pillow.

August 21, 2010

Saved by the Shoe

*G*rowing up, one of my New Year's resolutions was always "Help save the world." (After all, I am a Boomer. We all wanted to do that.) I started very small, with ants.

It happened this way. When I was in first grade, my mother made me wear Saddle Oxfords. If you grew up in the '50s, you know what they were and may have had the misfortune of having to wear them, too—big ol' clunky black and white shoes that made my skinny legs look even more like sticks. I've seen advertisements for them recently and cannot believe they are back in style. Run, children, run.

My mother said I had to wear them for arch support. What first grader wants arch support? Especially when your best friend's mother lets her wear red Keds to school every day. My mother wouldn't let me wear Keds because she said Keds did not have any arch support.

Not only did my friend get to wear red Keds, she also wasn't shy and didn't have skinny legs and freckles like me. The chips were definitely stacked on her side. All I had going for me was I was a fast runner, but not even the fastest—probably could have been if not for those clunkers, I told myself. But that certainly wasn't enough to make up for my other deficits.

When I went out to recess, I usually pretended to be a horse and galloped around the playground and over to my favorite ant bed. It was way out underneath the oak tree, far from the other kids and teachers. I always brought the little guys some of my Fritos. One of the good things about the '50s was that you got to take junk food out to recess. I imagined that the ants were very glad to see me. They were my friends and didn't ask me to talk. Shy kids appreciate that. We had our own little world, complete with snack under the oak tree most every day. Life was good.

But then one day a couple of bullies came over to see what I was doing and saw my ant bed. "Let's step on it!" they said.

"You can't," I protested. "They're my friends."

They just laughed. I quickly put the arch of my shoe over the bed to protect it, hoping it was high enough not to squish it. But that didn't stop the bullies—they stomped hard on my foot, but to no avail. I wouldn't move it. Finally, they gave up and ran off to find someone else to bully. The ants were safe, saved by the shoe, you might say.

I think that's when my future "save the world" drive must have been triggered ...except it does not extend to ants now, and I sprinkle their beds with poison every time I see them. (Please, don't tell the ants.)

I also learned I can stand up to pain and that good can come out of everything, even Saddle Oxfords. I mean, my friend sure couldn't have saved the ants with her Keds. Maybe they are not such a bad idea. Mothers—go ahead and buy your children a pair of those Saddle clunkers—just don't tell them I said so.

December 30, 2012

"Miracles"

A PRAYER FOR THE CHILDREN

YELLOWSTONE NATIONAL PARK

There was a little boy in my first grade classrooms years ago who never brought a pencil to school. "I'll bring one tomorrow, Mrs. Horne," he would say, day after day. Then one day he finally confessed, "Mrs. Horne, my mama don't have no pencils." I went home that night and wrote this poem for him and other little boys and girls whose mamas don't have no pencils.

Do you believe in rainbows
and new life from a barren tree?
Do you believe in canyons carved
by rivers that used to be?

Then you believe in miracles,
it's all possible, you see—
and when you believe in miracles,
you can believe in me.

Do you believe in the sea turtle's
inborn quest for the sea?
And the monarch's flight home
for thousands of miles,
or the honey that's made by the bee?

Then you believe in miracles,
it's all possible, you see—
and when you believe in miracles,
you can believe in me.

Don't say, "No hope, no way,"
that I can be set free;
for God can weave my life
into His beautiful tapestry.

All I need is a gentle hand,
A voice, a beacon in my night;
to lift me off and give me a push
and I'll soar toward the light.

For I am no less a miracle
than a rainbow, a monarch, or a bee.
I have gifts to be opened and shared
deep inside of me.

All it takes is someone to care,
someone to believe,
and someone to share.
Then I can believe in miracles too,
the miracle that is me—
loved by you.

1991

Promise

I had the best job in the world because I got to be there at the beginning—those precious moments of a child's life when he or she enters first grade. I saw the hope, joy, and love of life shining from their eyes. They dreamed big dreams.

Everything was fresh and new because they were still living at "Pooh Corner," that symbolic epitome of glorious childhood. "Counting bees in the hive, chasing clouds from the sky, and wondering how to loosen the honey jar from the nose of a bear," were the tasks of their days. All of life was an adventure for them and their *joie de vivre* was contagious.

My first graders saw things clearly. There is no one more insightful, poignant, smarter or funnier than a first grader. In first grade, almost all children come to school eager to learn, with a spark of curiosity that just needs to be fanned to burst into flame. At 6, life has not yet had a chance to dull their enthusiasm or make them believe they are not good enough or smart enough. Their gifts still have wrapping paper on them, just waiting to be opened.

For 20 years I taught in both economically disadvantaged and economically privileged schools. I found little difference in the children's brilliance or enthusiasm because those gifts follow no creed, color or economic background.

I felt like I had stumbled upon a little-known secret. Children from varying circumstances have the capacity to excel no matter where they grow up, what race they are or how much money their parents have or do not have.

At 6, everyone has promise.

I got to see that promise before life happened to some of them and it got snuffed out. I got to see their gifts and hear about their dreams before the children became silent and fell through the cracks of the very system that was supposed to save them.

How can we keep this from happening to our children? As their community, it is our sacred trust to help them, especially those whose parents are either unable or unwilling to do so. As my principal used to often say, "No child is a throw-away."

We need to create scaffolding for our children by nurturing and supporting them along their way. We need to create opportunities for them to succeed and keep that spark of eagerness and curiosity alive. We need to help fuel their imagination and spirit so they can continue to dream their big dreams.

Children are resilient, but they cannot go it alone.

Consider volunteering to read with an economically disadvantaged first grader. Become a "Forever Friend" for a grade school or high school student. Support the arts for children through volunteering or donating money. The list is as long as your imagination can stretch.

With the support of the community, someday their dreams just might come true.

August 15, 2009

"The Cracked Egg"

The child
trapped in the egg,
unseeing.... unhearing
unknowing.... unknown;
impervious to light and love
But slowly developing in the
egg, at first minute, but there,
yes, there..... a crack, timid....
but resolute. The ray of light
sought, found and slipped in,
a silent soldier destroying
the impenetrability of the
cruel fortress. The child
saw the way out...and
the egg CRACKED.
Hope was
Born.

Inspired by my children at G. K. Foster Elementary School, 1991-96, and written in honor and recognition of Dr. Martin Luther King Jr.'s dream.

1992

Don't Let Your Fear

BE YOUR GOD

*I*t's worse upon awakening, perching boldly at the edge of our subconscious, unbidden—our fear, waiting for us to acknowledge it. For the time being, still looking like a bad dream.

Our fear usually stems from that thing in our life over which we have no control. Maybe a death, a diagnosis of cancer, a loved one in the stronghold of mental illness, or perhaps the slow creeping demise brought on by dementia.

Sometimes, we can't even pinpoint why our fear is there.

Busyness and cluttered thoughts tend to keep it at bay during the day. But at night, when our defenses are down, fear creeps in and has free reign again. It tries to lure us to its lair, by deluding us into thinking there's nowhere else to go.

Our lives become oriented around our fear, and it eventually drags us into the swamp of despair and hopelessness, because we have let our fear become our god.

There is no solid ground in that swamp, only muck and mire, and we begin to sink. We find we can't carry the burden. Where once there was a future, now there's only a past. We can't look forward, only backwards. We feel alone in the dark night ... except for our fear, our constant companion.

We try to numb our fear, perhaps with a single-minded pursuit of pleasure, money, or stuff; or maybe with alcohol or drugs. But then they, too, become our gods, and we stay in the mire.

The good thing about being in the mire is we have to learn to be still so we won't keep sinking.

When we are still, we may hear the voice of the only true God, if we are listening.

When we are still, the veil between heaven and earth becomes just a little thinner, and we can sense God's presence more easily.

So we wait, not even sure what we are waiting for. And finally, the time arrives.

Through the muck and mire, we begin to see Hope emerging from the tomb, bringing with it the one True Light, Jesus Christ, our Lord and Savior.

Fear draws back and loses its hold on us forever, then silently slithers away.

Our hearts, minds and bodies now rest in God's hands ... without fear ... come what may, and nevertheless.

God can be our God, or fear can be our god.

But not both.

I waited patiently for God to help me; then he listened and heard my cry. He lifted me out of the pit of despair, out from the bog and the mire, and set my feet on a hard, firm path, and steadied me as I walked along. He has given me a new song to sing, of praises to our God.

—Psalms 40:1-3 (TLB)

December 11, 2010

Ode to My City

*Y*ou had me at the gas station, Longview. Twenty-six years ago when my family and I drove into town on U.S. Highway 80 from Dallas and stopped for gas, this amazing thing happened—people talked to us. That doesn't sound like a big deal unless you have lived in a city so big that people rarely meet anyone else's eyes, and shopkeepers only say what is necessary for their transaction to take place. I remember getting back in the car and saying, "Can you believe this?" to my husband. It more than made up for all the pickup trucks we saw as we drove in. (Nothing against pickup trucks, you understand—it's just that never seen so many; it's like they travel in packs.)

After living in the "Big D" for 11 years, my husband had received word that he was being transferred to your neck of the Piney Woods; so that first visit we looked for a place to live. It wasn't long before we found a beautiful apartment complex complete with a lake and ducks for our young daughters. Soon after we moved in, we found a great church, pediatrician and joined the Newcomer's Club, to boot. Six months later, we bought a house twice as big and thousands of dollars less than the one we had in Dallas. (It didn't hurt that our timing coincided with the bottom falling out of the housing market.)

Longview, we found out you have everything the Metroplex has to offer, but just one or two of everything instead of 100. I like that you narrowed them down for us. I mean, who needs more than one mall? That's why God made freeways—so you can drive somewhere else if you have a hankering for multiples. The fact that we can go out to eat and see a movie in about the same amount of time we would have stood in line for a restaurant in the big city is only one of the reasons I love you.

Yes, the Metroplex has nice cultural events, but you better not mind expensive tickets, long waits and being part of a crowd of hundreds. But *your* cultural offerings are also excellent, Longview. We can not only get in, but we can get involved since there are multiple opportunities for volunteerism here.

I didn't volunteer when we lived in Dallas because I was always in survival mode; most of my energy and efforts were expended on getting from place to place. My drive to and from work encompassed three major freeways—45 minutes each way was the rare best case scenario. That's another thing I really love about you, Longview. The "other side of town" is never more than 15 minutes away, and none of it is on a freeway.

But the part I love most about you, Longview, is what we discovered all those years ago at the gas station the very first time we set foot in you. Friendliness—it is your essence...your best thing. You are the "smiley-est" city I've ever seen. Smiling at everyone you pass in the store or on the street is unwritten etiquette around here. Why, people even smile at each other in the gym and elevators, which are normally the socially-accepted places to act like people standing within inches of you don't really exist.

On the walking trail I frequent, not only are smiles and greetings exchanged, I've heard more than a few over-achieving runners throw out actual short paragraphs as they dashed by—"Hope you have a wonderful day and great weekend." Where do they get that much breath? Only in you, Longview.

We've been spending a lot of time on the road between you and Forney, Texas, these days to help out with our 4-month-old twin grandsons. There's a billboard with the "Longview—Real East Texas" logo on it; it reminded me of the city-wide contest held a few years ago to choose your slogan.

Had I entered my choices, you could have been anything from "Longview—City of Smiles," to "Longview—Land of Love," to "Longview—the Face of Friendliness," or my favorite—"Longview—Basically the Best." Because that is what you are. We have been blessed to have lived and raised our family here and I can't think of anywhere else I would have rather have been.

Longview, you had me at the gas station...and I've never looked back. Thanks for the memories.

September 18, 2012

Plan B

*I*recently came across one of those gift shop coffee mugs which always have slogans on them. This one said, "Life is all about how you handle Plan B." Ridiculously over-priced, I bought it anyway. It struck a chord.

It has been my observation that Plan A's tend to have short lifespans, so it is definitely in your best interest to have a Plan B. You just don't want to use it, like life insurance.

When Plan A hits a rough spot, my default mode seems to be fear, anger or both. I can choose to stay in the swamp of destructive emotions and wallow in them, or I can choose to have faith that God will lead me to Plan B. Looking at the options not only spiritually but objectively, having faith is the only viable one I can see.

When God throws you a rope over the chasm of your circumstances and you finally decide to take hold of it, that's faith.

Following faith is hope, the kind that is grounded in eternity. Hope *without* faith is ephemeral. It is wishful thinking. True hope is a by-product of faith—the anticipation of what we know God is going to provide for us.

What He provides is not always what we want, but always what we need. We forget that God has the 10,000-foot view, and we have the 10-foot view. He is the Lord of the universe, and we're not.

God promised that if we believe in him and have faith, everything will turn out all right in the end, which is really only the beginning. He will use Plan B for his glory.

Even God had a Plan B when the Garden of Eden didn't work out—Jesus.

Therefore, since we are surrounded by such a great cloud of witnesses, let us throw off everything that hinders and the sin that so easily entangles. And let us run with perseverance the race marked out for us.

—Hebrews 12:1 (NIV)

February 9, 2011

Grand Canyon Love

The Grand Canyon. The very name fueled my 5-year-old sense of wonder. Its magnificence captured me the first time I saw it through my 3D View-Master. I could not conceive that there could be a more beautiful place on earth. It definitely took first place in my imagination, (which is what a 5-year-old has instead of a Bucket List.) Years later, it continued to inhabit my dreams but remained an unfulfilled desire.

This past spring, some 50 years of dreams later—there I was on a road trip with my husband, driving to the Grand Canyon down a seemingly endless highway through parched grassland dotted by small scrubby trees. According to our map we were close, but so far there was no sign of imminent magnificence.

We rounded a curve and suddenly, there it was. The earth had been cut away, leaving behind an unfathomable landscape of such power, immensity, and multi-faceted beauty that it took my breath away. My imaginings of the Grand Canyon had never even come close to this. Even though I knew what the Grand Canyon looked like, I really did not know it at all. There is a difference between seeing and knowing. The Grand Canyon must be experienced before it is known.

"Unconditional love" has a similar landscape—one of power, immensity, and multi-faceted beauty. It is "Grand Canyon Love." I used to think I knew all about it, but "knowing it" and "living it" are two separate things. Perhaps that is why God brought it to my attention.

In life we can see or hear something so many times that it ceases to have much significance. Then one day we happen to see or hear about it in a different way and the lens through which we view it changes. Suddenly, it is brand new again.

When rereading I Corinthians 13, (the "Love" chapter in the Bible) the thought struck me that Grand Canyon Love is not just something you *show* to a specific person or people—it is also a compilation of traits like patience, kindness, and loyalty. It also is *not* many things: jealousy, envy, boastfulness, pride, selfishness or rudeness. It is not irritable and does not demand its own way. It does not hold grudges and is never glad about injustice. And it never ends.

Maybe unconditional love is also a lifestyle, I thought—*a noun as well as a verb.* As I continued to reflect on the passage, however, I realized I was very much mistaken.

It came to me with a flash of clarity: *unconditional love is not a lifestyle—it is a life—Jesus'* life. *He* is love. And only from Him do we receive the fruit of His Spirit—all the "traits" of unconditional love. What an astonishing thought. The remembered realization of the miracle of God's gift to us in Jesus Christ changed the lens for me.

Jesus alone is the source of Grand Canyon Love. We cannot serve up this love on our own, like grilling steaks for a neighbor. We can sound good, look good, and never get so much as a speeding ticket but none of that is worth a dime if we don't have love. We can feed the hungry and house the homeless, but if we don't do it in love, then we are just a clanging gong or a crashing cymbal. How many times have I just made noise instead of truly loved?

Good intentions are not enough. Only by the power of the Holy Spirit are we able to share the unconditional love of Christ by being his hands and feet on earth.

The Bible doesn't suggest guidelines on who we should love because God made it really simple *and* really hard—everyone. We can't wait until we feel like loving because feelings do not count where Grand Canyon love is concerned. The bottom line is, "Love the Lord your God with all your heart and with all your soul and with all your mind, and love your neighbor as yourself." Even if your neighbor annoys you or cuts you off in traffic. Even if he walks down the street pushing a shopping cart. Even if he is a Republican, Democrat, black, white, brown or multi-colored.

Francis Chan (*Crazy Love*) said, "Our greatest fear as individuals and as a church [and as a society] should not be of failure, but of success at things in life that don't really matter."

Which is everything but love—*Grand Canyon Love.*

July 30, 2011

"Lost and Found"

A TALE OF REDEMPTION

*T*he girl could not remember a time when she couldn't look up from her front yard and see the tips of the Ferris wheel over the treetops. It was part of the fair—the one that was permanent at the state fairgrounds. It was rumored that the fair was not a nice place. She had heard of people who went to the fair, but she never did. Until that summer.

It was a hot, humid day and the girl sat in her front yard, bored. After a while she became aware of the faint sounds of the fair in the distance. She watched the tips of the Ferris wheel revolving. Her thoughts rested on it for a while. The girl wondered how it would feel to go to the fair and ride the Ferris wheel.

The following day she went again into the front yard, her gaze once more drawn to the Ferris wheel. Mesmerizing and intriguing...she decided that it would not hurt anything if she were to slip away and make a quick visit to the fair and ride the Ferris wheel.

Early the next morning the girl quietly left the house, determined to visit the fair and get back home before anyone realized she was gone. When she arrived at the fairgrounds, she saw that it was surrounded by a high stone wall. A guard leaned against the gate, casually cleaning his gun. It crossed her mind that she should probably turn around and go back home. But the girl didn't. Since she did not notice a ticket booth anywhere, she approached the guard and asked where she might purchase one.

He looked at the girl with dark, hooded eyes. "Come on in," he said with a smirk as he opened the gate. "You pay later."

Once inside, she quickly set off towards the Ferris wheel, the tantalizing sights, sounds and smells of the fair intoxicating her. As she got closer to the huge structure, she noticed the peeling paint on the support beams and the tangle of weeds grown up around them. Rusted chains clanged and creaked as the giant wheel groaned to a stop.

The girl's heart beat faster as a sense of foreboding crept over her. But she was so close—it was too late to turn back now, she told herself as she climbed on. The wheel started up again, turning slowly at first, straining, and then plunged into full throttle.

She reveled in the motion and speed and soon everything was just a blur. When the wheel stopped, the girl stayed on, not wanting the experience to end. After all, the guard said she wouldn't have to pay until later, and no one was keeping track of how much she rode.

After a while the thrill began to wear off and riding the Ferris wheel was beginning to make her feel nauseous. The girl decided she'd had enough and was ready to go home. After climbing unsteadily out of her seat, she headed back towards the entrance. Now she noticed how dirty everything looked. Funny how she hadn't seen it on the way in. Cigarette butts and crumpled cans littered the spittle-covered sidewalk. The girl couldn't wait to get out of this place.

Finally she got to where she thought she had come in, but the gate was not there. She looked around, disoriented. An old woman with stringy, gray hair was shuffling by. Trying to hold back a growing sense of panic, the girl tapped her on the shoulder. "Please ma'am, can you tell me how to get out?"

The old woman stopped and turned back around. "Didn't you know?" she wheezed. "There *is* no way out. That's the price you pay for coming to the fair." The old woman continued her slow shuffle, to nowhere, apparently.

"But I never wanted to live here, I just wanted to visit," the girl sobbed. A horrible realization struck her—she had thrown away her life for a ride on the Ferris wheel.

Sinking to the ground, the girl curled up in cigarette butts and broken dreams. The sun went down and the moon came up, but she did not notice.

Sometime during the long night, the girl became aware of what she could only later describe as a Presence beside her. She cracked her eyes open, or maybe she just dreamed that she did. It was dark, but the girl could see the Presence surrounded by a golden light. For some reason she was not afraid and a sense of being loved and cared for spread over the girl like a soft blanket. She closed her eyes again.

Then she felt a touch on her shoulder. She lifted her head and the radiant Presence was still there, only now she could see His face. Somehow she knew that He was good and that He could also see into her heart. Feeling the stirrings of something like hope, she tentatively ventured, "Sir, I want to go home." Her voice broke. "Can you please show me the way?"

The Presence smiled at her and opened His arms. "I have missed you so, child. Remember, I *am* the Way. In *me* is where you live, move and have your being, for you are My beloved child. I have never let you go, and I never will. Welcome home."

Jesus said, 'I am the way and the truth and the life. No one comes to the Father except through me.'

—John 14:6 (NIV)

1992

"The Call of the Unicorn"

When the world lost its color,
all things turned to black and white.
When the music no longer moved me,
day became an angst-filled night.

Then through the darkness beamed
a shimmering ray from a breaking morn;
and I glimpsed for a crystal moment
the face of the Unicorn.

So brief at first the vision,
I thought it illusion after all.
But the shimmering ray indelibly stayed,
so I followed the Unicorn's call.

It led me to a world
where still existed
the dew-filled morn;
and I heard again the music
by the grace of the Unicorn.

As we journeyed I begin to see
intimations of a new reality.
With doubts removed
and the way made smooth—
The veil was torn
and hope,
Reborn.

For Christ Himself is our way of peace.

—Ephesians 2:14 (TLB)

December 30, 2010

God is Good

*H*anging on our bedroom wall is a bright yellow canvas dominated by a big, green smiley-face heart. Its bold words proclaim, "God is Good." The simplicity of the statement belies the power of the message.

The artist was a homeless child at Newgate Mission. She painted it during the "Healing Art Project" held at the mission last summer, and I was fortunate enough to purchase it.

I wish I had met her. I wonder how, especially in her circumstances, she can already know that God is good? After all, her hopes probably don't even include presents on Christmas morning—just breakfast

How can she know that in the "moment"—that place where children live, move and have their being—that God is there, too, and is always good, no matter what.

Somehow this homeless child must have already caught a glimpse of this truth—maybe felt the brush of angel's wings or sensed the still, small voice in the storm whispering it to her.

I wonder why we sometimes forget this truth as adults. Perhaps we let it become clouded by failed hopes and dreams, or even by too many successes. Maybe it becomes dulled by the debris of misplaced priorities or a sense of entitlement.

How can she already know what can take some of us a lifetime to learn, and what others of us never learn—that God is good, *nevertheless and come what may.*

I heard those words from the pulpit of my good friend and former pastor, Dr. Bill O'Neal, every Sunday until he retired in the mid-'90s. Those words were powerful and filled me with the assurance of God's goodness.

41

Years later, my husband and I discovered the truth of those words when we went through the fire—our daughter's mental illness, and came out on the other side of it. Now, four years later, we are about to enter it again with my husband's recent diagnosis of early onset Alzheimer's.

Fire clarifies and rids us of our false sense of self-sufficiency. It brings us face-to-face with our total lack of control over our circumstances—health, prosperity, even life itself. We discover there is no "happily ever after."

But we also discover there's something even better—"joyfully ever after." Joy is not close to the surface and dependent on circumstances, like happiness is. Joy runs deep—soul-deep. It cannot be touched by anything of this world.

Joy is why the homeless child can say, "God is good." Joy is why *we* can say, "God is good."

Joy is the spring from which *"nevertheless and come what may"* flows, and the spring from which joy flows is Jesus—One who knew what it was like to be homeless.

JOY to the world, the Lord is come!

If the Lord is indeed our shepherd, then everything goes topsy-turvy. Losing becomes finding and crying becomes laughing. The last become first and the weak become strong. Instead of life being done in by death in the end as we always supposed, death is done in finally by life in the end. If the Lord is our host at the great feast, then the sky is the limit.

—Frederick Buechner (*Listening to Your Life*)

December 17, 2011

Seeing Jesus

We saw Jesus Christmas morning. Not in a manger scene or during a church service, but at Newgate Mission in Longview, Texas. We were there to help cook and serve breakfast, but instead we were served the "Bread of Life."

Because we saw Him in the faces of the struggling and the homeless, some with their clothes soaked all the way through from sleeping in the cold rain.

They came for their pre-breakfast church service and sat in hard metal chairs. We heard Him through their voices as they sang and prayed and offered thanks for being alive yet another day.

We saw Him as they reached into their pockets for the few coins they might have to place into the offering plate.

We witnessed His compassion through them as they reached out to welcome and embrace a young woman with unwashed hair and missing teeth who came in late. We glimpsed His reflection in her grateful eyes and smiling face as she relaxed into the warm blanket of His love extended to her through her community.

Because that's what they were—a community, ministering to each other in their brokenness, like communities are supposed to do. One where Jesus moves and heals. One that is grateful for the basics like shelter, food and life. One who prays, "Give us this day our daily bread," and means it.

Isn't that all we are supposed to really desire and ask for—our daily bread—not all the other stuff. That's what Jesus taught his disciples.

Some of us are so incredibly blessed that we tend to think only in terms of what we don't have. I know I do. Those who are less fortunate seem to be more thankful for what they *do* have, like a place to come in out of the cold and rain.

Perhaps the less one has, the thinner the veil. Instead of "six degrees of separation" from God, perhaps there are just one or two. Sometimes it seems all of our blessings block "The Way."

Yes, we received a priceless gift on Christmas morning—the eyes, just for a moment, to see the Christ child incarnate in His people, and in a most unlikely place. Kind of like being born in a manger.

God, please give us the grace and discernment this Christmas and New Year to remember to look past our blessings and see You.

Help us to remember what we do have instead of what we don't.

December 31, 2011

Becoming Light-bearers

There are now more than five million people in the U.S. diagnosed with Alzheimer's disease. On November 9, 2011, my husband became one of them.

At least, we told ourselves after the diagnosis, we already knew the drill for catastrophic illnesses, since our daughter suffered from a severe mental illness when our first grandson was born five years ago. Although it was an extremely scary and traumatic time, we were blessed with God's grace and love along the way. He had been there with us, and we knew without a doubt He would be there this time, too.

Now, four months later, the Alzheimer's diagnosis is still unbelievable at times. We cycle back and forth through the stages of grief: numbness and denial, anger and resentment, guilt and regret, depression and despair and at times, some degree of acceptance. I guess that will go on awhile.

I have been surprised at what some people have chosen to share, although I'm sure they meant well. A few have expressed to me that Alzheimer's is a "living hell" and warn that we are "entering a nightmare." I have no doubt that the pain and suffering are tremendous, and I have much sympathy for those who have experienced or are currently experiencing that depth of pain.

But right now we need to hear about grace and hope—any kind. I reminded myself that surely God can be found in the midst of the pain—somewhere, somehow. After all, He promised.

Please God, I prayed. Let me see you. I will try to remember to keep my eyes and heart open, especially as the darkness deepens.

Then, through the newly-formed Alzheimer's "Trailblazers" support/education group, His reassurance came.

At the first meeting we met an eloquent couple who were to become our role models for how to live with Alzheimer's. "Bob" is a distinguished and eloquent man who was diagnosed about seven years ago. He and his wife radiate love for each other and God's hand in their journey became immediately apparent as they shared it with us.

They said it better, but it went something like this:

"We are viewing this disease as a curve in the road, not the end of the road. We view it as an inconvenience. It is part of our lives but not the center of our lives. We seize every moment. We laugh, have fun, and enjoy each other to the fullest. God is good."

Wow. It makes all the difference in the world when you find "light-bearers," those people who are walking or who have walked the broken road and will remind you, "It will be OK. God's joy will be with you, and He will carry you through the pain. Through Him, you can persevere."

We are coming to realize that although this is our story, the disease should not be the main idea and neither should we. The main idea is not what happens *to* us, but what happens *through* us. Will we live in such a manner that God can use us to become vessels of His love and light? Will we allow our life circumstances, both the blessings and the trials, to draw us closer to God, or push us further away? Will we live well the story we have been given?

Everything else seems beside the point.

February 11, 2012

An Unshakable Kingdom

I discovered there were baby birds in our fern last spring when I accidentally watered their mother. She flew out squawking and scared us both to death. After that I started watering just around the edges. Then I would pull the fronds apart slightly and peek in to check on my two little peeps. Their mom provided their food but I kept their shelter alive, so I felt like kinfolk. One day I looked in and they were gone. Just like that—no five-minute warning or anything. *Please come back and at least let me say good-bye,* I silently implored.

I was struck by an intense sense of loss and started crying, all the while wondering what on earth was the matter with me. I don't usually cry easily, (except when reading books and watching movies that have redemption in them and…OK, maybe I can't make that claim.) However, I cried more in those ten minutes over the suddenly-departed fledglings than I did when my daughters left for college. (Please don't tell them that.)

It finally dawned on me—this empty nest became symbolic of all loss to me—and more basic than that—of my utter lack of control. Perhaps lack of control is what we would find at the bottom of our fears if we picked them up and looked underneath. Because if we had control, we would have no loss. If we had no worries about loss, we would have no fear. We would have…everything…perfect. And we would also be God—who has everything perfect—but us. In Him, however, we are made perfect, He says.

It seems to all work together, like an equation. I was never good in math, but this is simple enough even for me to grasp. God is good that way—making it simple so we can all understand; yet, we still find a way to make it hard. As a former first grade teacher, I can just imagine God wanting to say, "Can't you please just listen and pay attention?"

Well, He did—He sent Jesus. "Can you hear me now?"

We don't have control ourselves, but we are to have faith and trust in the One who does.

My husband and I experienced that truth, once again, a few weeks ago. Our daughter, pregnant with twins, was hospitalized after she went into early labor at 31 weeks. For four days she was hooked up to IV fluids and monitors as measures were taken to try and stop the contractions and keep her and her baby boys safe.

On her second day in the hospital, the contractions became worse and she was put on a stronger medication which had bad side effects. But that's not all. It was also the day that multiple tornadoes rampaged across north Texas. In the hospital room we watched as live coverage showed a tornado tossing 18-wheelers in the air south of Dallas. The storms continued moving east and one of the tornadoes headed towards our hospital where our daughter lay hooked up to an IV and monitors. As the sirens went off, yet another one of the tornadoes headed toward the community where my daughter and her husband live.

There was nothing to do but sit there in our utter lack of control, and pray. Overriding our fear was the calmness and peace that passes all understanding—knowing that no matter what, all would be well. God has the "Big Plan"—not just the five-year or the 10-year, but the infinity version. And we know that "In all things God works for the good of those who love Him, who have been called according to His purpose (Romans 8:28 NIV).

Who can separate us, indeed? We are part of a Kingdom that is unshakable.

Therefore, since we are receiving a Kingdom that cannot be shaken, let us be thankful, and so worship God acceptably with reverence and awe, for our God is a consuming fire.

—Hebrews 12:28, 29 (NIV)

April 21, 2012

Taking a Stand

Now, since our condition accommodates things to itself, and transforms them according to itself, we no longer know things in their reality; for nothing comes to us that is not altered and falsified by our Senses. When the compass, the square, and the rule are untrue, all the calculations drawn from them, all the buildings erected by their measure, are of necessity also defective and out of plumb. The uncertainty of our senses renders uncertain everything that they produce.

—Michel de Montaigne (*The Essays of Montaigne*)

I had to learn the hard way, as usual. I was pretty sure I had read all the directions before I started wallpapering our kitchen, quite competently for a first-timer, I thought. Honestly, I don't remember reading anything about a plumb line. (I also have to admit I didn't know what one was.) The paper *looked* straight until I got about halfway around the room. That's when I found out how absolutely essential a plumb line is…if you don't want to take the paper down and start over.

Perhaps that is what our culture needs now—a big, long plumb line to keep us on track when we are tempted to turn on "The Bachelor." We have become a nation of voyeurs and tend to default to whatever is in front of us—celebrities, sports, reality shows, movies, Facebook, slick advertisements, gossip magazines—the list goes on. We are becoming too lazy to make the effort to dig deeper. It is scary when the mores of popular culture so heavily influence our moral climate that, "If it makes me happy, then it must be OK," has become our national mantra.

Look at the stars we are following and the lives they lead; look at the themes of casual sex, foul language and gratuitous violence in popular TV shows and movies that we're not only watching, but internalizing. It is disturbing, especially in light of the studies on brain plasticity that show how the brain changes and rewires itself in response to the stimuli it receives.

Are we also losing our ability to experience a healthy "cognitive dissonance" about our behaviors? Are we simply changing our beliefs to justify our actions? It is so much easier to just go with the flow. But if we don't constantly line up against the plumb line, everything becomes relative. Then there is no right or wrong, good or bad—it is just whatever we want it to be. That is the most frightening scenario of all.

The unspoken message of, "Everyone is doing it," and, "Things are different now," implies that we are somehow now under a new moral law. Who gave the OK for that?

Maybe we did.

Maybe, by not taking a stand or speaking up in order to avoid offending anyone, anytime, anywhere—we gave the impression that it was all fine with us.

Sarah Young (*Jesus Calling*) put this in perspective, however. "Fear of displeasing people puts us in bondage to them and gives them tremendous power over us. Pleasing others becomes our primary focus instead of pleasing God. And we cannot serve two masters."

Changing our actions, speaking up, and making a difference all require making an intentional effort that must be fueled by the power of the Holy Spirit, or we will follow our natural inclination to avoid conflict. At least I will.

All we are asked to do besides receive His grace is to share it.

God's Holy Word is our plumb line. If our walls are not vertical, our house will collapse.

Take a stand—for God's sake.

For God has not given us a spirit of fear, but of power and of love and of a sound mind.

—2 Timothy 1:7 (KJV)

June 9, 2012

The Safest Place on Earth

Even the natural heart of the unsaved will serve if called upon to do so, but it takes a heart broken by conviction of sin, baptized by the Holy Spirit, and crushed into submission to God's purpose to make a person's life a holy example of God's message.

—Oswald Chambers (*My Utmost for His Highest*)

*I*n our society we are taught that we must be whole, healthy, vital, energized, self-actualizing individuals in order to realize our full potential. But God's ways are different from ours. He says that only through our brokenness is He able to work and bring us to our full potential in Him.

When looking through the Bible, you begin to notice how things are broken before God works through and uses them—culminating in Jesus' body being broken for us, through which came the ultimate wholeness.

A number of years ago at "Meet the Teacher" night, a new first grader walked through my door. She was different from the others. Her clothes were dirty and bedraggled; her hair, unkempt. She did not possess the usual light and bounce of a 6-year-old. The woman with her impatiently explained to me that she was the little girl's aunt and was raising her now since she had been abandoned. The little girl, oblivious to the aunt's irritation, shyly raised her eyes to me and handed me a brown paper bag.

"Teacher," she said, "I have a gift for you." Her aunt added, "Oh, it's just some old thing I gave her; I don't know why she wants to give it to you." I reached in and pulled out a heart-shaped box covered with red satin. Although it was stained and worn, I think it was one of the most precious gifts I had ever received. And I realized the significance—my new little first grader had given me her heart for safekeeping.

We approach God in our brokenness much the same way. We all must reach that point where we hand Him our broken and stained hearts and say, "Here, Father, keep this safe for me. It's yours."

How does God work His healing miracles in our brokenness? In my life He did much of it through spiritual community. Dr. Larry Crabb, (*The Safest Place on Earth*) defines a spiritual community as "a safe place to hit bottom."

Crabb writes that spiritual community begins in brokenness, and the death of brokenness only happens in a safe community. Its purpose is to draw people to Christ, to mirror Christ to one another, and to show Christ to each other.

"There we can experience the life of Christ poured into us by God through His Spirit," said Crabb. "We hit bottom only when we find the safest place on earth."

June 14, 2012

From the Beginning

From the beginning
I knew I had married
an artist,
an actor,
a comedian
and a musician.

Then I found out
I had also married
Elvis,
Santa Claus,
BeeRon the Clown
and the Easter Bunny.

But now I know
who I really married—
A Warrior.

He is still all those
things and more
while fighting with faith
and steadfastness
the silent enemy.

A Warrior—
from the beginning.

June 17, 2012

"Sometimes I Can't See God"

Not in the big things, anyway.
I feel overwhelmed,
but then I hear a word
or a song,
and I remember
to wait on Him.

For He will come
once again.
I will see His face
once again.
In the meantime
I will praise Him
while I'm waiting.

I will look for Him
in the small things.
I can always see Him there—
a leaf, illuminated by sunlight;
a grandbaby, sleeping;
or a flower surfacing
through the weeds.

The small things—
conduits of grace
when framed by our focus,
reveal our Father's glory.
And then He comes,
once again.

June 22, 2012

A Marvelous Mystery

God reveals himself to us throughout our day, leaving room for us to recognize him or not. Every now and then his revelations are startling instead of subtle. I experienced him in one of those startling ways soon after my husband was diagnosed with Alzheimer's on November 9, 2011.

For a short while, Byron and I skimmed along the surface of our new reality, trying not to think much about the unwelcome guest in our lives. However, we needed to dive into the myriad legal and financial decisions and paperwork that had to be synced with this new reality.

Reluctantly, we began the job and were promptly overwhelmed. Dealing with reality also meant that we both truly had to accept the fact that Byron had Alzheimer's. The load was heavy.

It happened during the middle of the night a few weeks later. Something stirred me, and through half-opened eyes I saw a golden light illuminating a Presence at my bedside. A feeling of peace and being loved and cared for enveloped me. My eyes began to close again and at the same time, I sensed a hand reaching out, and then felt a firm touch on my shoulder. "What?" I asked a now-dark room as I sat up, wide awake. Nothing. *Just a dream.* Disappointed, I drifted back to sleep.

The next morning, I woke up with an immediate recollection of the dream/event in great clarity. I turned it over and over in my mind, examining it from all angles. With growing delight, I realized that of course this was God's doing. Even if it was, indeed, *just a dream*—it was still a marvelous mystery of a dream that God used to remind me of His loving care.

Maybe I would have missed it, except for the touch.

I used to scoff when I heard or read about things like this. It's not that I didn't believe God could show himself anyway He chose; it's just that I was skeptical.

But God's ways are the ways of faith. They cannot be proven or explained. So I gratefully accepted this gift for what it was—a glimpse of Grace. It served to strengthen me for the journey, and I hold it in my heart.

Life itself can be thought of as an alphabet by which God graciously makes known his presence and purpose and power among us.

—Frederick Buechner (*The Alphabet of Grace*)

July 16, 2012

Dem Dirty Dembangers

*M*y Aunt Kathryn is 84 years old and classy. She looks and acts much younger and still runs her own oil company. I admire her greatly, and have always been just a little intimidated by her sophistication and intellectual prowess. I consider her my second mother.

Sometimes she'll ask me to show her things I've written. Awhile back she read a few of my pieces, then commented, "Dorothy Marion, (my mother was a Dorothy too, so I always had the Marion tacked on) your writing has improved." I felt a warm glow, but before I could bask in it, she continued, "I'm so glad you're not using all those tacky exclamation marks anymore."

Oh. I had hoped she hadn't been aware of my dirty little secret. For years I have been trying to kick my exclamation mark (aka dembanger, bang, interbang, screamer, gasper and startler) habit. Its various names sound like illicit drugs, come to think of it. My favorite is dembanger—*How 'bout dem bangers? Well, who dat?* (Sorry, my Louisiana roots.)

Ironically, I'm a dembanger snob as far as my own reading material goes—if I come across one in a novel, I will close it in a huff, bristling that some author would waste my time by injecting his book with amateur perkiness.

But, life feels so dull and boring when I'm just using periods. Of course there are always smiley faces and LOL's. However, they don't fill the void.

Yesterday I wrote a note to Aunt Kathryn, thanking her for treating us to a delicious lunch recently. As I read back over it, however, I was mortified to notice I had placed an exclamation mark after every…single…sentence. How could I have fallen so far, so fast?

I guess those dembangers grab hold of you again in little increments—one here and one there on Facebook, a few more slipped into emails and you are on your way down the slippery slope again. Meanwhile, you are still telling yourself that you have things under control. But one day you turn your back for a few minutes and they jump in, full throttle, and start popping up everywhere, like fire ant beds in East Texas.

I considered a minute, then instead of rewriting the note and purging those dirty dembangers, I just added a PS:

Oops!! Just noticed all the exclamation marks!! So sorry, Aunt Kathryn!!

I know when to raise the white flag.

July 9, 2012

Join the Fight

TO CURE ALZHEIMER'S DISEASE

*I*t was the early '70s and I was in college. My roommate and I would sit in our dormitory room and talk for hours about "The Meaning of Life" with the Moody Blues' classic "On the Threshold of a Dream" playing in the background.

Because that's where we were—within spittin' distance of the dream—"Real Life." I figured it would start after I got out of college and would never have to study for another test.

What I found out, of course, is what we all find out—there are indeed tests in Real Life, only harder and with much more at stake. The one I am taking now is the hardest—watching someone I love lose himself to Alzheimer's. And I can't even study for it...just live it.

However, my husband's test is harder than mine since he is one of the five million people in the U.S. who has Alzheimer's, and one of 36 million worldwide. So far, it is a fatal disease with no cure.

This year the National Institutes of Health will provide $5.45 billion for cancer, $4 billion for heart disease and $3.1 billion for HIV/AIDS. The Institutes plan to provide only about $500 million in research funding for Alzheimer's disease.

This year, it will cost $200 billion to care for those with Alzheimer's in the U.S., mostly in costs to Medicare and Medicaid. According to George Vradenburg, president of USAgainstAlzheimer's (a national advocacy group), the disease will also be "...a driver not just of health issues, but a driver of our ability to control our national deficits and debt." The group maintains the disease must become a national priority, or the U.S. will be overwhelmed with as many as 16 million Americans with Alzheimer's by 2050, at an annual cost of $1 trillion.

Even so, Marc Wortmann, executive director of Alzheimer's Disease International, said there is still little response from governments in improving services and putting money into Alzheimer's research despite the huge costs "because of the stigma."

Because of the stigma? Alzheimer's research and funding doesn't get as much response because of the stigma? That is outrageous.

The World Alzheimer Report 2012 said about 25 percent of people with dementia reported trying to conceal their diagnosis and 40 percent say they are excluded from everyday life because of the stigma. Those diagnosed with Alzheimer's and their families shouldn't also have to deal with negative connotations and lack of understanding, nor should funding suffer because of the stigma. What a sad commentary.

The National Alzheimer's Association says that more than 100 research studies pertaining to Alzheimer's and related dementias are currently underway and recruiting volunteers. However, recruiting and retaining trial participants is now the greatest obstacle to developing the next generation of Alzheimer's medications other than funding, the organization says.

Last May, the U.S. launched the first National Alzheimer's Plan, which set a deadline of 2025 to find a cure for the disease. The last major breakthrough was in 2003—too long ago.

None of us can do it alone. Please join the fight to find a cure for Alzheimer's disease. Let's raise awareness, educate the public, advocate for those suffering with the disease and eradicate stigma. Let's work to convince lawmakers to earmark more money for Alzheimer's research.

There is no more time to waste. The clock doesn't stop ticking for people with Alzheimer's disease, or for those who don't have it yet, but will.

We cannot afford to pretend it's up to someone else anymore.

September 28, 2012

Fighting Alzheimer's

THE LAB RAT WAY

*I*t used to be that being Elvis, or Santa, or a clown was enough. Not anymore. Now my husband is a "lab rat wannabe." For Alzheimer's, no less. He got his first gig last week in Big D at Texas Neurology.

So he and his roadie (me) went for part one of a three-part screening exam to see if he qualifies to participate in the IVIG (Immune Globulin Intravenous) Phase III drug trial. It will take about six weeks to complete the three parts, assuming he is not ruled out at some point.

We had always heard drug trials were hard to get into and usually involved weekly travel and lots of medical tests and procedures. We heard you had to be willing to commit a good deal of time and energy to it, so we weren't interested in pursuing a trial when Byron was first diagnosed a year ago. We would wait and see how things went. Maybe later—in the meantime, he had his other gigs.

But now that we've been on the Alzheimer's road a year, we are realizing we cannot really take "having more time" for granted. So why not use part of that time by trying to do something to extend it?

We began investigating drug trials in the surrounding areas and found two or three possibilities in Dallas. After initial phone interviews, we decided to try for the IVIG trial, which included approximately 400 people in regions around the world. The drug itself has been used for more than 25 years to treat a variety of immune deficiency and autoimmune diseases. At the end of the study (probably sometime in 2013) the hope is that the FDA will approve it for treating Alzheimer's, also.

The first screening was a great experience, thanks to the staff at Texas Neurology. It includes multiple doctors and clinical researchers who are all are involved in various ongoing drug trial programs involving diseases of the brain, nerves, muscles and spinal cord. Our doctor specializes in Alzheimer's and other memory disorders.

He and the clinical research manager spent a lot of time with us and were patient, respectful and compassionate—explaining everything thoroughly and in layman's terms, and soliciting questions along the way. (We felt like we were in doctor's office heaven.) Byron also had an EKG, X-Ray, and blood tests, along with a memory and thinking skills test; altogether we were there about three or four hours. Soon we will know if he qualifies to go back for a second screening. If he passes that one and the final screening, he will become a part of the trial for the next 18 months.

Now that we're "doing something," our journey has more the feel of an adventure instead of a death march. Alzheimer's may be a "Goliath," but now we may have a "David."

Granted, Byron may not get in, or if he does, he may get a placebo (there's a one in three chance.) However, we know that if he himself does not benefit, somebody down the line will.

The goal of the study is to "evaluate the safety and effectiveness of the medication and see if it is able to change the rate of memory decline and daily functioning in subjects with mild to moderate Alzheimer's disease." In some of the drug trial literature, the caregiver is referred to as the "study partner" and the patient is the "subject." (I suppose it is nicer than being referred to as the "lab rat." At least the cat will not want to play with you.)

Flashback: revised marriage vows: "Will you take this man to be your Subject? And, "Will you take this woman to be your Study Partner?"

Just goes to show—you never know where love will lead you. But you do know, at least, that God is already there.

November 14, 2012

Jesus in Disguise

I'm thinking back to one of the best days I've ever had; it was around this time last year. I was on my way to the Family Dollar Store to pick up some Christmas wrapping paper and bows, when suddenly people in passing cars began to smile and wave at me. I smiled and waved back, cheered by this unexpected Christmas merriment. When I got to the store, the occupants of yet another car rolled down the windows, yelled "Merry Christmas," and gave me a thumbs-up. I walked across the parking lot, and garnered even more smiles and waves.

Before I entered the store, I stopped and looked around one more time to see if anyone else was waving at me (I could get used to this). Seeing no one, I went in and lo and behold, smiling mothers and children begin to point at me and whisper. A few even shyly sidled over to tell me what they wanted for Christmas.

I guess I better go ahead and admit it—I wasn't myself that day, I was Mrs. Claus. Also, I suppose I need to confess that the "Big Guy" was with me. We had just finished a gig, and maybe a teeny bit of all that attention I received was because of him.

Anyway, when the children started coming up to me in the store, I realized I better put my shopping list on hold. I wasn't sure what the protocol was for Mrs. Santa and her shopping habits, especially when children were present. For instance, was it OK for Mrs. Santa to be buying Christmas wrapping paper and bows at the Dollar Store in Longview, Texas? Is that something she would have done, or is that something the elves would have taken care of at the North Pole? Surely that would be an elf job.

I did not want to be the one responsible for destroying any expectations the children may have had about the mysterious

Santa and Mrs. Claus, remembering how precariously balanced and short-lived those expectations are in the fleeting years of childhood.

Ah, Santa—I guess we should have known better, but I really hadn't wanted to go back home and shed my persona along with my red dress and become simply me once more. This must be how movie and rock stars feel. What a letdown to have to become yourself again after having all that adoration lavished on you for appearing to be someone you are not.

It sure was a fun few hours, though. I remember thinking, "Wow, if this is how people treat a fake Santa and Mrs. Claus when they run into them, what would they do if they saw *Jesus* walking down the street?

Oh wait, we *do* see the real Jesus walking down the street, every day in the faces of the poor, the needy, the hurting—and in the faces of you and me. But He is so easy to miss—unless you are seeing him with your heart.

Jesus is here...He is just in disguise.

For I was hungry and you gave me something to eat, I was thirsty and you gave me something to drink, I was a stranger and you invited me in, I needed clothes and you clothed me, I was sick and you looked after me, I was in prison and you came to visit me.

Then the righteous will answer him, 'Lord, when did we see you hungry and feed you, or thirsty and give you something to drink? When did we see you a stranger and invite you in or needing clothes and clothe you? When did we see you sick or in prison and go to visit you?'

The King will reply, 'I tell you the truth, whatever you did for one of the least of these brothers of mine, you did for me.'

—Matthew 25:35-40 (NIV)

November 26, 2012

"I Should Have Brought a Stone"

I should have brought a stone.
You should have brought many things, he thought.
But you did not bring them, old man.
Now is no time to think of what you do not have.
Think of what you can do with what there is.

—Ernest Hemingway (*The Old Man and the Sea*)

Sometimes I think
I should have brought a stone.
Maybe it could have helped me
navigate my way through the chaos
that ever threatens to close in.

Maybe I could have stayed
brave and upbeat
and encouraging and helpful—
all those things that are so hard to do
when you are empty.

Maybe, if I had brought a stone,
I would still be able to hear the music.
God, where is the music?

Then God said,
"Think of what you can do
with what there is.

You don't have a stone—
you have a Rock."

Because you are my help, I sing in the shadow of Your wings.

—Psalm 63:7 (NIV)

December 3, 2012

A "Real Man"

What is a "real man?" It is one of those popular questions that society occasionally tosses around for its amusement. Used to be a real man was one who drank a certain kind of beer or smoked a certain kind of cigarette. Now real men seem to be football players (before they get busted), reality show stars (before the ratings go down), or politicians (before they get investigated.)

However, *my* vote for a "real man" goes to my husband, because he embodies courage—defined as "the ability to face danger, difficulty, uncertainty, or pain without being overcome by fear or deflected from a chosen course of action." That is him for sure.

This real man is walking courageously into his destiny with his head held high and trusting in God. He is a man with a servant's heart and a zest for living; one who thanks God every day for his many blessings. He adores his family and enjoys the simple things—playing with his grandsons, taking his dog for walks, laughing, making jokes, singing, playing the guitar, entertaining and generally making life fun for everyone around him.

This real man is not letting Alzheimer's get the best of him, not as long as he still has any say-so in the matter.

Alzheimer's is not something Byron and I focus on or talk about usually, but I asked him if he would mind sharing some of his recent thoughts and feelings with me so that I could share them with you. We both feel it is important to be open and honest on this journey as we continue to share our story with others, trusting that God will somehow use it for His glory. So he talked and I recorded, and here are his (mostly) unedited comments. You can hear the angst, and also, you can hear the hope. Through it all, you can hear the courage.

You were diagnosed a year ago. What are your feelings about having Alzheimer's now?

Alzheimer's is something I would not wish on my worst enemy. It takes away one of the things that is most precious to me—memories. Also, I feel isolated at times. I feel immobilized at times, and that's not me. I don't like to doubt myself and wonder, 'Did I remember this? Or did I forget that?'

It's something that I try not to dwell on because it gets me all tied up in knots. I'd like to know that there is something I can do. I want to have a way to deal with this rather than just sitting there and accepting it. You feel so helpless when there is no way. I want to keep on going; I want to keep on trying.

What can people say or do to help?

I'm thankful for people who are willing to be with me as I go, and who understand. If I look like I'm not quite sure who you are, tell me—'Hey remember me, I'm so and so.' That will work just fine. Names are really tough for me to keep a handle on, and I hesitate to ask people their names because they probably have told me. The pressure can really get to you when you're trying to remember a name.

I try not to dwell on what's wrong. I get reminded of that enough as it is by forgetting. I don't talk much about Alzheimer's; it's not that I'm ignoring it; I've just chosen not to dwell on it. It's something that I accept, but it doesn't have to be at the forefront. There are other things I can think about.

What helps you get through it?

I wait. And, I keep moving...keep going. The number one thing that helps is my relationship with God—my faith, knowing that all the things that have happened to me were under the guidance of God. I have a deep faith—that, above everything else, is the thing that I cling to. Then there's family—you, our children, our grandchildren—you are all part of something to hold onto. So I just immerse myself in family. All that doesn't have to be part of this disease.

It's a struggle to be normal. I'm still learning. There comes a point in which I have to say—OK, this is just the way it is. I don't like it, but I can't stop it and I'm not going to give up. I want to take advantage of every opportunity I have to not only deal with it [Alzheimer's] personally, but to help other people who are going through it the best that I can.

What do you consider your legacy?

I've got four grandsons. I've got two daughters and two sons-in-law. I've got you, and we have been with me through the good times and now we're going through the not-so-good times. My legacy to them is that I care about them, I love them and I thank God they are there.

My legacy to pass on is this—have faith. There is a way. I can't say that I understand everything, but that's what faith is for—when you don't understand but know that you'll be getting through it, because it won't be just you. It will be God and you.

December 11, 2012

Your Past Will Follow You

RIGHT TO THE BORDER!

BUTCHART GARDENS IN VICTORIA, BRITISH COLUMBIA—2012

*Y*ou hear lots of stories and drama about "border crossings" these days. Now I have one. It all started when I purchased two packets of flower seeds—the kind you can buy at Walmart. All that happened afterwards on the ensuing unfortunate day at the border made me realize I must have made it to "The List." You know, the one they use at airports and borders to help prevent questionable characters from wreaking havoc.

I suspect it is because they found out I know how to fire a bazooka.

It was something I learned for my Riot Control class as college freshman law enforcement major. I confess I also know how to throw tear gas and do a pretty mean step-thrust with a riot stick into an unruly crowd. (I was known as "Dirty Dot" around the dorm.) Riot Control was one of my most fun and useless classes ever. (Later I switched to education, so my riot control skills eventually came in handy when I became a first grade teacher.)

Anyway, that must be how I got on The List. I should have known my checkered past would catch up with me someday. What I didn't know is that apparently because of me, my three traveling companions (husband, former college roommate and her husband) also got on the list. We have always considered ourselves to be the pretty clean-cut, boring types; a retired state employee, a retired Army Colonel, a retired first grade teacher, and a director of a non-profit agency. (We are not talking "Born to be Wild" here.)

Recently, the four of us decided to take one of those vacations on our "Bucket List"—a trip to the Pacific Northwest. We flew to Seattle, rented a car and explored marvelous mountains, rain forests and beaches in the Olympic National Park area. Then we hopped a couple of ferries to visit beautiful Victoria and Vancouver in British Columbia.

One of the highlights for us in Victoria was touring Butchart Gardens, which is what I imagine a huge Garden of Eden would look like, without the snake. I decided to take back a reminder and on the spur of the moment bought two little packets of flower seeds on the way out of the gift shop. It was the only thing I bought on our whole trip (except for a new jacket to take the place of the one I accidentally dropped off a chair lift.) Actually, it was the only purchase made by any of us on the trip, I think. We spent all of our money getting there; plus we are just cheap.

The first intimation of trouble came when the cashier rang up the seeds. "This will be $2.47," he said. "I'm going to put your seeds in this bag with a special sticker on it, and don't open it. When you go back across the border, hand it over with your passport to declare."

I told him never mind, that I really didn't want to have to declare anything. "I just won't buy them," I said.

"Oh, it'll be no problem—it's just a routine thing," he assured me. (Don't ever believe sales people, even over $2.47.)

So I paid for them and we went on our merry way for a few more days, then drove back towards Seattle so we could catch our return flight. Arriving at the U.S.–Canadian border, we joined the long lines of cars waiting at the booths. We finally reached a border guard and I obediently handed over my passport and two packets of seeds, still in their bag with the seal unbroken, just like the store clerk told me to do.

"Oh, you have seeds," he said apologetically. "I'm sorry, but you will need to park your vehicle at that building over there and go in—all of you." I offered to throw the seeds away instead. "Oh no, it's no big deal," said the guard. "It should only take about five minutes."

"Oh, let's just do it," said everyone but me. "It's part of the border experience." (Trust me, you don't want a "border experience.") We should have remembered that three different "random alarms" went off when we went through security screening at the beginning of our trip; and three of the four of us were pulled aside to receive "pat-downs"—in retrospect, a foreshadowing of our security troubles to come.

Inside we found even longer, winding lines to the various border agents. An official asked us what we had to declare and we were directed to the man who was to become our nemesis—Herr Border Guard. "So you have something to declare?" he asked in an accusatory voice.

"Yes sir, two packets of flower seeds valued at $2.47." My companions and I all smiled. Not him. (Word of advice—do not ever smile at border guards.)

"You all seem to think this is funny," he said. Well, yes, we kind of did, we admitted.

He then proceeded to very seriously remind us about all the illegal stuff that could come over the border, bringing with them diseases, fines and jail time. We nodded in agreement—we could understand that, being upright, law-abiding U.S. citizens. Since we knew he did not like smiling and could not see the humor in our seed situation, we tried our best to look earnest.

That was not good enough for him, although the seed packets had passed right away with flying colors. Apparently, we were still due an interrogation—where had we gone, what had we done, what had our occupations been before retirement and what else was in our car and suitcases. I blurted out that I left a half-eaten sandwich in the door pocket, hoping desperately it was not illegal because I could see our relationship with Herr Guard was extremely precarious now. I fully expected him to ask where our firstborns lived next.

Then my friend had to go and get busted again by smiling.

"You still seem to find this amusing," he said to her. He enunciated each word slowly and distinctly. Then, "All of you need to take a seat, and give me the keys—I want to search your vehicle."

Seriously? I mean—we weren't in a third world country or illegally crossing a border or drug smuggling or anything. Although we had absolutely nothing to hide (we were pretty sure), by this time we were more than a little nervous about what he might come up with (or plant) in the car that could warrant putting us in the slammer, since he had alluded to it several times already.

After all, we suspected we weren't in reality anymore, but had somehow entered a "theatre of the absurd." My husband said later it was like we had walked into a "Monty Python" sketch—only we weren't laughing, at least not anymore.

Personally, I think it was more like "The Twilight Zone." And I wanted to get out before the ending. They were never good.

Eventually we were allowed to leave. I guess Herr Border Guard felt he had sufficiently subdued us. (The good thing is, we can now scratch "border experience" off of our Bucket List.)

Young people, your past will follow you. Remember that.

September 10, 2012

"A Fresh Palette"

"It's snowing," the children said.
"It's snowing," the people told each other.
For awhile, at least until the snow melts, all is right with the world.
The noise, clatter, and clutter are covered over;
the ugly, the dirty, and the darkness itself—mercifully hidden.
The chaos of human-contaminated creation lies undetected
beneath the whiteness of a fresh palette.

The people held their breath, and felt almost new.
Please, they whispered to God—let it last just a little bit longer.
Please.

And God whispered back...
"My people...Hope is born today...did you not hear?
Hope is born today.
For I have sent My baby boy
to save you from the darkness.

"The old has passed away and all things are made new,
not just whited out or hidden or undetected.
For My Son has trumped the noise,
the clatter and the clutter, the ugly and the dirty.
He has trumped the chaos of human-contaminated creation.

"He alone can give you a fresh palette
and make you whiter than snow—
For He has trumped the darkness."

Then cheers of great joy and exceeding gladness
arose from the people as they remembered.
"Hallelujah!" they shouted.
"Glory to God in the Highest.

"For Jesus, the Son of God, is born today.
Our Prince of Peace, our Savior and our Lord."

And they promised never to forget again….

And there were shepherds living out in the fields nearby, keeping watch over their flocks at night. An angel of the Lord appeared to them, and the glory of the Lord shone around them, and they were terrified. But the angel said to them, "Do not be afraid. I bring you Good News that will cause great joy for all the people. Today in the town of David a Savior has been born to you; He is the Messiah, the Lord."

—Luke 2:8-11 (NIV)

December 27, 2012

Seeing Through Eyes

OF FAITH, NOT FEAR

*A*lzheimer's—I know what I don't want to do this New Year... spend it worrying about what you will do and where you will take us over the next 12 months. I do not want to dwell on those things you've already stolen, for then I would be letting you rob us of something you otherwise would be powerless to take—the time we have now. I am not letting you have it, Alzheimer's.

This New Year I resolve to embrace this journey we are on and stop seeing life through eyes of fear but through eyes of faith, like a child. I want to look upon each day we have together with anticipation, joy and a sense of wonder—remembering that the time spent in it will be precious. I want to see past the unloveliness of the disease and into the beauty of it, appreciating the opportunity to love and support unconditionally from the inside out—with my whole heart, mind and soul.

I want to give God praise and thanks in all things instead of wasting my time and energy fearing you, Alzheimer's. Ultimately, you have no power over us. Only our Father does, and He will provide. He will be our Strong Fortress and you will not win.

Don't be afraid, for I have ransomed you; I have called you by name; you are mine. When you go through deep waters and great trouble, I will be with you. When you go through rivers of difficulty, you will not drown. When you walk through the fire of oppression, you will not be burned up—the flames will not consume you. For I am the Lord your God, your Savior, the Holy One of Israel.

—Isaiah 43:1-3 (NLT)

January 1, 2013

A New Year of Hope

"THE YEAR OF THE LAB RAT"

For us, this New Year brings boundless hope, for it is "The Year of the Lab Rat."

Byron went through three screenings in the fall to see if he qualified to be part of the drug trial for the immune therapy treatment called IVIG/Gammagard, which he did. That means for the next 18 months he will be an official Lab Rat. (I see a possible new reality series—"I Married a Lab Rat." It could happen...there have been worse.)

We went to Texas Neurology in Dallas yesterday for his second infusion of the drug. He sat in a big, comfortable leather chair hooked up to an IV for three hours and watched a movie on his DVD player, while a nurse brought him margaritas (oh wait—that part was just in his dreams.) All went smoothly, just like his first infusion experience before Christmas. The second experience was even better, Byron noted, "because I learned to bring my own entertainment."

He has a one-in-three chance of receiving the full dose of the drug (but one is better than none.) The other options are a half-dose or a placebo—no one knows for sure what he's getting but the pharmacist. Scientists have called the drug "probably the most exciting one we know about that is currently in the late stages of research." In a previous small study it was shown to prevent or slow decline in cognitive skills and memory. Scientists think the treatment clears toxic proteins (beta amyloid) from the brain, allowing brain cells to function properly. The test will be to see if the initial result in the small group can be replicated in this larger study group that Byron is in.

The infusion room has about 18 chairs along the perimeter and a nurse's station in the middle. People come and go, and most of the chairs stay filled. Various diseases are being treated and everyone is friendly and upbeat. Some are conducting business on their laptops while others are chatting with their neighbors, talking on the phone or sleeping.

The woman sitting next to us on our first visit had been a patient there for years and comes weekly. She said her infusions take about eight hours since the medication has to go in slowly because of the side effects. In passing, she mentioned that her daughter was scheduled to have an organ transplant the next day. It reminded me that other people are enduring much more than meets the eye.

We go back to Dallas next week for the third infusion, and after that Byron will get to have them in Longview. A home health nurse will come to our house and do the infusions every other week and we will go to Dallas every three months for memory and cognitive skills testing.

People ask us, "So how are you doing?" Mostly we say, "Just fine," because it's true more and more of the time. That is, if we're remembering to trust in God's provision and live "independently of our circumstances" by keeping His perspective in our lives. Then life is good, because our God is good.

Be anxious for nothing, but in everything by prayer and supplication with thanksgiving, let your requests be made known to God; and the peace of God, which surpasses all understanding, will guard your hearts and minds through Christ Jesus.

—Philippians 4:6, 7 (NKJV)

January 10, 2013

The Lab Rat Saga Continues

*I*t reminded me of something out of *The French Connection*, kind of. A few days ago, a smuggler (disguised as a FedEx employee) driving a Lincoln Continental (disguised as a FedEx truck) delivered to our doorstep a box containing a drug allegedly used to treat Alzheimer's. It was wrapped in plain brown paper and accompanied by three large boxes which were also wrapped in plain brown paper. They contained the drug's assorted paraphernalia and equipment. We had been given strict orders by the "Big Boss" *not to touch anything*, and that our contact (disguised as an infusion nurse) would arrive shortly after the boxes did to open them. (The dog and cat provided the obligatory chase scene.) It was all quite mysterious.

But back to reality.... (can it really be reality if the drug costs up to $5,000 and sometimes more, per infusion?) Unfortunately, yes. It has a very short shelf life and is delicate, which is why it gets special treatment and shipping privileges. That, and the fact that it is so hard to come by are several of the reasons why it's so dang expensive. A whole lot of people have to give a whole lot of blood since the drug solution (intravenous immune globulin) is made from the pooled plasma of thousands of healthy blood donors. It has been used for years to treat many immune and inflammatory diseases and now, with its potential for use in treating Alzheimer's, the demand is even greater.

After our boxes were delivered, the infusion nurse from Plano, Texas, arrived right on schedule. He was a Korean gentleman and very polite, professional and efficient. After introducing himself, he wasted no time in opening the box and removing the drug from its cozy chilled interior. It needed to sit out precisely 90 minutes before being hooked up to the Lab Rat. I'm not exactly sure why, but I think it was in order to get to room temperature in addition to probably gathering its powers.

During the wait time, the nurse set up all the equipment and soon a corner of our den looked somewhat like a small hospital room, only with a dog, cat and a big screen TV. Right on the money and not a minute before, Lab Rat was hooked up to the IV. Afterwards, the nurse did some paperwork and talked with us a bit. We found out that he contracts out to do infusions statewide with two companies, and also runs his own infusion service company. Most of the infusions he performs take hours and involve daily travel, sometimes quite a distance away. No matter what, however, he goes home to Plano every night. "For my children," he said. That's the kind of man he is.

Three hours later the infusion was over. It was a tight, impressively run operation. Before our nurse left, (I can say "our" because we found out that he'll be doing Lab Rat's infusions for the remainder of the study. We are thankful.) He asked us where in our house would be a good, safe place to keep the equipment until next time.

That included a needy IV pole contraption that has to stay plugged in all the time or it will die (and it goes without saying that, of course, it is also very expensive.) Then it will have to be shipped back to its supplier or the Big Boss or whoever and exchanged. We think we found a safe place with a plug, but will only know for sure after the grandchildren come to visit.

As he was leaving, the infusion nurse turned and gave us a slight bow, because that's the kind of man he is. It felt like a benediction.

February 6, 2013

Byron's "Top Ten" List

HOW TO LIVE WELL WITH ALZHEIMER'S

*S*ometimes God calls us to do something we never would have chosen. We ask, "Why me?" A better question would be, "What is being asked of me?" Byron is being asked to do something he can only do with God's help, and that is live well with Alzheimer's disease. In the end, it is a sacred journey as all journeys are for those who seek His kingdom. It will be different for each person, but most likely it ain't gonna be Easy Street, as they say.

Byron's thoughts:

I don't know everything about Alzheimer's. In fact, I feel I know practically nothing. I want to be an encourager, but I'm certainly not a sage. I'm not the old man on the mountain who has all the answers. I can accept the disease, but I don't have to enjoy accepting it, if that makes any sense. Also, I don't really like to call it a 'journey' because it makes me sound so noble. And, I don't like to think I'm going anywhere.

I don't want to be defined by this illness. I just want to be considered a regular person, not 'Byron—that guy with Alzheimer's.' OK, that's all my 'don'ts.' The fact is we were given life but not promised that everything would be perfect. The important thing is we have a God who loves and we have a God who provides. It's just that we're not in charge of the schedule of when and how those things are provided.

Below are his "Top Ten" observations and suggestions for others who may find themselves on the same road. (I didn't say "journey.")

1. *There is help available if you want it.*

2. *Remember, you're not the only person dealing with Alzheimer's.*

3. *Stressing yourself is the worst thing you can do when you've forgotten something.*

4. *Feed your mind as well as your stomach. Find memory games on your computer and play them daily.*

5. *A keyboard is not an exercise machine. Take your dog for a walk. Take yourself for a walk.*

6. *Ask for directions.*

7. *Stay active. There are clubs and organizations you can become involved with.*

8. *You've learned a lot over the years. Find a way to teach it to someone.*

9. *Keep living, keep loving. Be happy. Trust God.*

10. *Make your own "Top Ten" list to share with somebody.*

February 14, 2013

Boomers, Bomb Drills and Such

Fifty years ago—yes, I remember. We were in the hall in "tornado drill" mode—face down, hands covering our heads. But in this instance, we were practicing protecting ourselves not against a force of nature, but the threat of man. It was 1962 and I was a third grader at Arthur Circle Elementary School in Shreveport, Louisiana.

This was a nuclear-attack drill, a daily occurrence during the 13-day Cuban Missile Crisis—the closest the world has ever come to nuclear war. I remember not being especially worried—a tribute to the calmness of my teacher and parents, obviously. To me it was like an adventure of sorts—stocking our lockers with cans of Metrical and water, "just in case" we had to stay in the school building a few days in case of nuclear attack, they told us. *Oh, OK,* I remember thinking.

Since Barksdale Air Force Base was just across the bridge in Bossier City, in all likelihood we wouldn't have had the chance to drink that Metrical and water. Barksdale, I recently found out, was the Soviet's No. 3 target, right after the Pentagon and Cheyenne Mountain. I am really glad we did not know that back then.

After the crisis was averted (thank you, John Kennedy) our school added a new curriculum so the teachers could warn us—a lot, about the dangers of being infiltrated by Communists. We began to fear there were Communists lurking in the hallways, under our beds and in our closets, just waiting to take over our impressionable young minds. Next to spiders, I feared Russians the most.

However we "Boomers," for the most part, seem to be a resilient bunch—being the generation who grew up breathing our parents' second-hand cigarette smoke and not wearing seat belts. My father traveled for a living, and my mother and I accompanied him. I spent the first five years of my life riding all over the United States while standing between my parents in the front seat of their car, smoking their cigarettes by default, and having their arms thrown across me at every stop. A kid has never been so glad to get out of a car.

When I started first grade, we settled down in Shreveport and I spent every summer, along with other neighborhood children, indulging in our favorite pastime—riding our bikes behind the mosquito fogging truck when it came by spraying out big grey clouds of DDT. "Fog Man's coming!" was the excited refrain heard up and down our street when any of us heard the familiar rumble approaching.

Everyone hopped on their bikes and waited to fall in line behind the "Pied Piper of Poison." The Fog Man was the highlight of our week, and no one's parents seemed the least bit concerned. What blissful ignorance. (We also rode our bikes up and down the rows of a nearby cotton field after the crop dusters flew over because we liked the smell of insecticide. But that was just plain stupid and we knew it. Even ignorance has its limits.)

How are any of us Boomers still alive, anyway? I don't know—maybe we could have taken on the nuclear fallout after all....just as long as they kept those Russians away from us.

Thank God we didn't have to.

October 30, 2012

Please Walk Across the Room

*I*magine being in a room full of laughing, chatting people who are speaking in a language you know but now find hard to follow in a large group. You stand quietly off by yourself, hoping no one will notice you. Lucky for you, no one does. But luck and tragedy walks hand and hand here. Alzheimer's is a cruel, isolating disease. What if someone had just walked across the room?

I have noticed that Byron deals with this problem on occasion now, even as social as he has always been. After coming home from a recent gathering, he commented, "I'm feeling more like an observer than a participant sometimes—just watching the people around me talk." It was one of those gut punches the disease delivers on occasion.

People mean well, but many are not sure of how best to communicate with a person who has Alzheimer's. Here are a few good ideas I came across on the website, Caring.com, entitled, "How to communicate better with someone who has early stage Alzheimer's."

These suggestions are useful mostly with the early to mid-stages of the disease.

Stick to familiar, easy-to-understand topics, too. A person with Alzheimer's or other forms of dementia is less likely to be confused if you talk about his favorite subjects or things he's demonstrated he remembers or relates to well— the weather, what's for lunch, the birds at the feeder, a ball game.

For Byron, forget the birds at the feeder or even a ball game— the best topics would be his grandchildren, our dog, music, TV shows, movies, and more about his grandchildren. (You could very well just leave out the other topics.)

Another way you might need to alter your usual conversational style is to stick to common, plain words and short sentences whenever possible. Try to construct sentences that include only one main thought, ask only one question at a time, and give instructions one step at a time.

Expect to carry the conversation yourself. It's not that the person doesn't like to chat, but initiating talk can be too much now. Also avoid asking too many open-ended questions, which may feel like "tests" of their memory....

I'll forget and do this more often than I would like to admit. "Who was at the meeting?" I'll ask Byron, or "What did your sister say when she called?" It's best to lead the discussion by providing information rather than asking for it. You can talk about yourself or your family or something you have in common. This gives the person with Alzheimer's a chance to comment or ask you questions, and they are not pressured to remember anything.

Above all, have realistic expectations. Even early on in the disease process, someone with Alzheimer's may occasionally use the wrong word, get confused, or forget what was said just a few minutes ago.

Basically we treat someone living with Alzheimer's exactly how we would want to be treated if it were us, which it might be someday. Have patience, value the individual as a person, and avoid seeing him or her as a victim. When people are considerate in this manner, Byron feels less anxiety and is assured that the darkness of the disease has not overtaken him.

Reach out to someone living with Alzheimer's; you may be the one that makes all the difference.

Please, walk across the room.

February 21, 2013

"I'm Rich at This Table"

"I'm rich at this table." Struck by the simple wisdom of the statement, I knew it was too good to go unremembered. It was a child who said it, of course. He had already figured out that life is a matter of perspective. Children tend to be unadulterated philosophers with astute observatory skills. I've noticed that as a rule, only adults are adulterated—tainted by the world's expectations as well as their own.

I overheard the line a few days ago at a local elementary school. The students got to bring money from home and shop at the Book Fair, which was held in the school library. It had been transformed into a virtual treasure cove for the children. Along with a marvelous array of books were posters of dragons, wrestlers and puppies, pens that wrote with invisible ink, erasers that looked like iPhones and many other fun items to amuse and distract each other with in the classroom.

The source of the overheard sapience was a pleasant fourth grade student who came in the library with his class when I was manning the adding machine for the purchases. He tried to buy three books with his $20 but discovered it was not enough. After putting a book back, he went to look for other enticing bargains and found a table overflowing with inexpensive items ranging from 50 cents to about $3. It didn't take long for him to realize he had hit the jackpot. After perusing all of the offerings, he picked out an eraser and came over to pay for it. I gave him his change and he looked at it with delight, then turned around and went back to the table to browse some more. He found another item, bought it, and still got change—so back to the table.

His good fortune continued through at least three more purchases. One of his classmates took note of all this and said, "Wow, you sure have a lot of money."

"Yes, I am *rich* at this table!" he assured his friend.

I love that line. If you think about it, we are all "rich" at different tables—perhaps family, friends, jobs, avocations, health or the like. However, there is one table that is absolutely priceless that none of us can afford—the table of Jesus Christ, the Lord of Hosts. But because of His marvelous grace, we don't have to—the price has already been paid. Jesus invites us to join him at the Great Feast and experience the exquisiteness of Life everlasting.

We are all rich at His table.

While they were eating, Jesus took bread, gave thanks and broke it, and gave it to his disciples, saying, 'Take and eat; this is my body.' Then He took the cup, gave thanks and offered it to them, saying, 'Drink from it, all of you. This is my blood of the covenant, which is poured out for many for the forgiveness of sins.'

—Matthew 26:26-28 (NIV)

February 28, 2013

When the "To-Do's"

BECOME THE "NOT-YET-DONE'S"

*S*ometimes it happens—my "to-do" list becomes more of the anxiety-producing "not-yet-done" list (which are to-do's that have hung around too long.) The not-yet-done's swallow every surface and empty space in the house as well as my mind and I feel like I am in a swamp. Unfiled papers, unpaid bills, unreturned phone calls and unanswered emails drive out what should have been my living, breathing, happening "now" life. At these times it becomes too easy for the specter of Alzheimer's to sneak through the back door, where it always lurks.

I remind myself to focus on "one bird at a time," like author Anne Lamotte suggests. But when a whole flock of birds is clamoring for attention, where do you start? I have often wished I could be more like my husband. He's one of those people with a linear, organized mind who completes one project before beginning another, and never feels the weight of what is yet undone.

On the other hand, I tend to have many swirling thoughts and a global, distracted mind. I feel the weight of everything I need to do all at once. Before I realize it, there are too many commitments made and projects begun and not enough time.

Fortunately, God gave me writing to help reframe and focus my thinking since, thankfully, only one thought at a time can emerge through a pencil or keyboard. Through this clarifying process, I can more easily see where my priorities are out of whack—like when my 'to-do's and' not-yet-done's have, in a sense, become idols and dominate my life.

Through writing, I can frame either the blessings or the trials—the choice is mine. May God grant me the wisdom to choose to see my circumstances through His eyes and strength and not my own.

Lord, when doubts fill my mind, when my heart is in turmoil,
quiet me and give me renewed hope and cheer.

—Psalm 94:19 (TLB)

March 8, 2013

Trial by File

One of my favorite things is thinking about organizing (not actually doing it.) I love to go to Walmart and browse the organizational aisle because therein lies the secret of the universe for me—the wonderful array of containers, file trays, pencil holders, folders, dividers, and notebooks that are just waiting to change my life. I confess to having a number of these items at home, as yet unused, but always decide to buy more as surely that will increase my odds of finally getting organized. I take them home; then I start trying to decide what should go in them. That's the hard part.

It goes like this—should I put this stack of papers in file folders or in a notebook? If so, which one? The 1-inch binder or the 3-inch binder? What should go in these containers? Maybe the file folders? Or perhaps books and notebooks? And what should I put in the file trays? (Papers, of course, but which ones?) What differentiates those that go in file trays as opposed to those that go in notebooks or file folders?

Complicating the decision is that I really need to "see" everything and if everything is neat and orderly and put away, I can't see it. On the other hand, one cannot have her whole life just lying around the house, although one can try.

After wearing myself out trying to decide what should go where, I resolve to think about it tomorrow, like Scarlett. In the meantime, I resort back to my default organizational style—the "pile" method. It's easy and fairly effective, until I wake up one morning and find they have proliferated overnight. Then it's like trying to get rid of roaches. As a last resort I call the pile exterminator (my husband.) He usually gets them all, but grudgingly. If any remain, it's just a matter of time before they take over again.

My other default organizational style is my favorite—the "laying-everything-all-over-the-floor" method—in a neat way, of course. That way I can see it all. The only thing is, this method has a very fragile eco-system. If it has to be disturbed because company is coming, the system will be destroyed and will have to be rebuilt, paper by paper. But more than likely the papers will just end up merging into a colony and become incognito.

I'll admit I used to pay one of our daughters $5 just to organize the bathroom drawer. I think she was in kindergarten at the time. She could fit all the pieces in the drawer like a puzzle, just like her dad; they are two of a kind. In fact, Byron has all his tools hung on the wall of our garage, like a big modern art puzzle. For years it has been the centerpiece of our home—men and women alike gaze at it in awe. My other daughter and I are also two of a kind—we are the writers and artists, we tell others and ourselves. That's our story and we are sticking to it.

Since all of this organization stuff really is in the genes, then I cannot help myself. I claim no responsibility and accept none. I just married the gene carrier.

March 21, 2013

Standing in the Gap

FOR SOMEONE WITH ALZHEIMER'S

So many wonderful people said, "Please let us know how we can help," when the news got out that Byron had developed early onset Alzheimer's. Then, I didn't know what to say. Now, over a year down the road, I do.

When a person has memory loss, their lives are made up of moments, not days. "We are not able to create a perfectly wonderful day with those who have dementia, but it is absolutely attainable to create perfectly wonderful moments," writes Dr. Naheed Ali in *Understanding Alzheimer's: An Introduction for Patients and Caregivers*. "As social creatures, people crave companionship and require regular interaction with peers….Therefore, when faced with a loved one suffering from Alzheimer's disease it is important for family members to nurture that kinship and for friends to stay supportive." To contribute to an improved physical state and less stress, he suggested surrounding those with Alzheimer's with "positive, upbeat, and emotionally supportive people….What is important is that the person develops a continuous and positive emotional connection with them."

They need people to be there for them—to stand in the gap for them.

So now when someone asks me how they can help, I have concrete suggestions to offer. I knew the time had come to begin calling on friends and family when Byron had to stop driving. Naturally, Byron was upset and depressed because it was a big loss for him, as it would be for anyone. When someone with Alzheimer's has to stop driving, their independence is taken away. They may feel isolated, forgotten, and no longer important. Staying active and connected to people is crucial.

Some of the ideas below might help you know how to stand in the gap for someone dealing with Alzheimer's.

Pray for the person with Alzheimer's—that they will have strength for the journey and continue to have faith and find meaning and joy in life.

Call occasionally just to ask how they are doing and let them know you're thinking about them. Or send a card—this will give them something they can go back and read again.

Invite them over to help you with a project, yard work, or anything. The important thing is they need an opportunity to serve.

Drop by and talk, or take them out for coffee or lunch. Invite them to movies or concerts.

Invite them to do just about anything that allows them to get out of the house and around people. For instance—run errands, take the dog for a walk or work out.

There will also be times when the caregiver is unavailable to be with or drive their family member. Let them know if they can put you down as one of the people they can call.

The bottom line is, those with Alzheimer's need people around them. They need to know others care so they won't feel like they are walking the path alone. Pray about how God may be calling you to help, and look for opportunities. We are blessed to have friends who are standing in the gap for Byron in so many ways.

Henry David Thoreau wrote, "To affect the quality of the day that is the highest of arts." Affecting the quality of someone else's day—I call that *Kingdom Love*.

April 5, 2013

"Hope Floats and He Reigns"

It was right after I heard about the Boston Marathon bombings. I was walking along the wooded bike trail with a heavy heart when I happened to notice something—fresh dogwood blossoms (sometimes viewed as a symbol of the Cross) floating in a pool of stagnant water. There was not a dogwood tree nearby. Unanticipated, it served as an epiphany that no matter what— Hope floats, and He reigns.

A putrid bog
of evil and terror;
but there, inexplicably,
Hope floats.
Not under it,
but on it.

Triumphant over all,
floats Hope—
The scum in its thrall.

God is our refuge and strength,
an ever-present help in trouble.
Therefore we will not fear, though the earth give way
And the mountains fall into the heart of the sea,
Though its waters roar and foam
And the mountains quake with their surging.

—Psalm 46:1-3 (NIV)

April 18, 2013

Giving Thanks in All Things

People ask, "Isn't it hard writing about personal things in your life for every-one to read?" The answer is yes, sometimes. But my words will mean nothing if I am not honest and transparent to the extent that I can be. We are all broken creatures and God is in our brokenness, binding us together. Our words can help each other. My prayer when I write is always that God might use my humble words to encourage someone and bring glory to His name.

⸺

*B*eing a caregiver for a loved one with Alzheimer's is like the two of you being stuck on an elevator—one that only goes down. It will stop on a floor and stay there awhile. You finally adapt to that floor, and living life on an elevator becomes easier, for the time being. You even forget you are on one, sometimes.

Then one day without warning, the elevator again begins its slow, inevitable descent. You panic, and hope other people will see it going down and do something, anything, to help you get off.

Finally it stops, and the adapting begins all over because the floor has changed. However, adapt you must and appreciate where you are, because now is as good as it will get.

Sometimes it is harder to be brave now. Sometimes Byron feels more alone, and I feel more overwhelmed. Sometimes I rage at a disease that shows no mercy. I know during these 'sometimes' moments, I am supposed to pray and ask God for help. But some-times, I just don't want to—it feels too hard. It is so much easier to slide towards the pit.

But, nevertheless...there's always a "nevertheless," and it is this—we *must* give thanks. We are *commanded* to give thanks. We *live*

to give thanks and praise Him in all things. Even in Alzheimer's...
even in death.

Ann Voscamp (*One Thousand Gifts*) writes, *If I only thank Him
when the fig tree buds—is this 'selective faith'? Practical atheism? What
of faith in a God who wastes nothing? Who makes all into grace? To give
thanks in everything is to bend the knee in allegiance to God, who alone
knows all. To thank God in all things is to give God glory in all things. Is
this not our chief end?*

*When I only give thanks for some things, aren't I likely to miss giving
God glory in most things? Murmuring thanks doesn't deny that an event
is a tragedy and neither does it deny that there's a cracking fissure straight
across the heart. Giving thanks is only this: making the canyon of pain into
a megaphone to proclaim the ultimate goodness of God. Our thanks to God
is our witness to the goodness of God when Satan and all the world would
sneer at us to recant.*

We hold on to His promises and we give thanks. Though we may
not understand, we are called to be faithful and know that God will
guide and sustain us through everything by the power of His Holy
Spirit.

In Him, we can persevere.

*Rejoice always, pray continually, and give thanks in all circumstances; for
this is God's will for you in Christ Jesus.*

—I Thessalonians 5:16-18 (ESV)

May 6, 2013

Stripping Down

TO THE MAIN THING

*L*ife is a "stripping down" process when you're living with Alzheimer's. We are trying to make the change from "too much and too many"—possessions, commitments, errands, and busyness—and learn how to live slowly, to be still and listen, and to stay in the moment. Moments become very important in the Alzheimer's journey.

Stripping down gets rid of the non-essentials which take up the moments and leaves only the essence. I wonder about the essence—what is the gold that remains when life is culled?

It has to be love because, "God is love. Whoever lives in love, lives in God, and God in them" (I John 4:16 NIV).

You can't get more basic than that.

Also, "Love the Lord your God with all your heart and with all your soul and with all your strength and with all your mind; and love your neighbor as yourself" (Luke 10:27 NIV).

You can't get more all-encompassing than that.

It is not just the casual kind of love we sometimes toss out like so many Mardi Gras beads, but unconditional love—the kind you can only receive through the power of the Holy Spirit. The kind that produces joy, peace, patience, kindness, generosity, faithfulness, gentleness, and self-control. If that's what life is all about, why do I let everything else get in the way?

I act like I've got so many more important things to do first. In the meantime, I forget the clock is ticking and I still haven't gotten to the main thing, and who knows when the game will be over?

Then I realize, I've forgotten to simply ask God for the main thing. Without a doubt my life needs to be culled, but first and more importantly—my heart. Nothing else matters if my heart is not purified from the dross of pride, impatience, anger, selfishness and all those other things that take up the space where the pure gold should reside—unconditional love.

No wonder it has been so hard—I've been forgetting to make the main thing, the main thing.

Create in me a pure heart, O God, and renew a steadfast spirit within me.

—Psalm 51:10 (NIV)

May 20. 2013

Are You Siri-ous?

I thought she was going to be my friend. I had always heard nice things about her, and how smart and helpful she was. It was just a month ago when she and her iPhone kingdom set up residence with us. I had always wanted someone around who could tell me all the answers about life and the universe... (no offense, Byron, but you had your shot!)

Well, ha. Now I know the real Siri—snobbish and controlling. Definitely on a power trip. In all fairness to her, how could she not be with millions calling on her daily for help and guidance? I'm sure she has way surpassed Heloise and Dear Abby, and probably Oprah and Dr. Oz, too.

Apple should know better than to put a woman in a phone and give her free rein with her opinions and advice. Next thing you know she will be consulting with the House and Senate about the government shutdown. Or maybe she already has; that would explain everything

But how will I ever find out anything if she won't admit to understanding my questions?

Personally, think it's a control thing, and not just with questions. For instance, yesterday my iPhone camera, for no apparent reason, refused to take a picture of an interesting patch of grass along the walking trail. Same thing with a beautifully-sculpted dead tree and a particularly striking weed.

Apparently Siri thinks she can decide when my subject matter is worthy of a picture. Things like lakes and mountains pass, but the small wonders—grass, dead trees and the like—do not.

I know she's behind it, being the self-appointed "Boss Lady of the iPhone." Looks like the camera and all the apps are under her thumb.

I can almost imagine her channeling my mother's voice when she thought I was doing something she considered ridiculous. "Oh, for heaven's sake, Dorothy Marion," she would exclaim in exasperation. Years later my daughters would echo the same sentiment with one word. "Mommm," they would say with exaggerated inflection to convey, "How can you do this thing that has the potential to embarrass me greatly?"

This never happened with my non-Siri model iPhone. We have got to have a serious talk, me and Siri. That is, if she can stoop to admitting she understands me.

The problem is, no matter how slowly I talk or try to sound like a Midwesterner, she always asks me to repeat—several times. After two or three times, I just give up. My accent is combination East Texas and Louisiana, and this is as good as it's gonna get, Siri. I consider her condescension a form of discrimination.

Am I mistaken or does anyone else detect a slightly sarcastic tinge to her voice when she says she "doesn't understand?" Does she really think having a snooty mechanical robot voice means she's better than me?

I'll bet she is the kind who never goes to Walmart. Siri probably carries a designer purse and shops at the most expensive stores in the iCloud mall. She more than likely watches reality TV and considers them intellectual pursuits.

I thought when I got out of Junior High, I would be done with people like her.

That's OK. I'll show her. I'm just going to shut her down and she can go back to wherever in cyberspace she came from.

That is, if I can figure out how to do it. I suppose I'll have to ask her.

And, of course, she won't understand me.

And so I'll be stuck with her. But, she will also be stuck with me—serves her right.

October 6, 2013

"A Remembered Sweetness"

Walking along the trail
I am accompanied by
a remembered sweetness
permeating the air and
carrying me back to childhood
and moments strung together
like pearls.

Simple moments,
glorious moments
and abundant moments
filled with the joy
of being alive.

A remembered sweetness
carrying me back to
two little daughters
and sharing their moments—
simple moments,
glorious moments
and abundant moments
filled with the joy
of being alive.

Turn the page
and four little grandsons
now share their moments—
simple moments,
glorious moments
and abundant moments
filled with the joy
of being alive.

June 2, 2013

Making a Difference

WHILE LIVING WITH ALZHEIMER'S

*T*he drug trial Byron has been participating in for the past six months was recently discontinued. Baxter International, Inc., announced the Phase3 IVIG Gammagard drug trial failed to meet its goals of reducing cognitive decline and functional abilities in a majority of patients with mild to moderate Alzheimer's disease.

Byron continues to persevere with a sense of purpose, faith and humor while living with Alzheimer's disease. I asked his permission to record his thoughts and feelings about the trial and how he continues to live life with Alzheimer's. Hopefully his remarks will benefit and encourage others with the disease, as well as their friends and family members.

Byron's thoughts:

I'm glad I participated in the trial because I felt I was making a contribution. I was part of something that was going to make a difference and mean a lot to many people I'll never meet. Every one of the drug trials are designed to see what's out there. I know if something is finished it could be for a variety of reasons, none of which is within my control.

After the trial ended the first thing I thought was OK, what next? What opportunities do I have now? My doctor assured me they plan to have other trials starting up in the fall, and he'll be in touch with me to see if I'm interested in participating. I feel pretty good about that, and I want to be there to help.

I've learned over and over if you do things for yourself, just to benefit yourself, it's kind of an empty thing to do. Yes, you may get something, but are you helping somebody else too? There have been so many people who have helped me that I have become very conscious of giving. If there's anything I have or someone else sees that I have to give which could be of benefit, whether it is drug trials or playing the guitar, I'm willing to consider it.

We all have something we can do to help other people. We may not think there is not any real value in it, but its value is when it is put into effect. It can be something as simple as sending someone a thank you note for a kindness they've done. We're not only told to help each other, it is in Scripture and it's common sense as well.

Alzheimer's does get your attention and prods you to start thinking about doing things that will not only benefit yourself, but others you know and those you may never know. There are too many people trying to look for things to take rather than to give, and a philosophy like that never leaves you satisfied.

We don't live out here all by ourselves. There's a lot of wisdom in "paying it forward." You don't do something to make yourself feel better; you do it because someone has done something for you. You know how it feels to receive, and we are called to give back. I have been blessed to know people who have given me opportunities to give back.

I wish the Alzheimer's wasn't there, but wishing about something or complaining about it and keeping a bad attitude over something you have no control over is a useless thing. It burns your energy and your attention as well as your feeling for your fellow man. A negative attitude doesn't get you anywhere other than where you already are. I would like to contribute instead of complain and feel sorry for myself.

We all still have something, even if something has been taken away from us. I can still walk, I can still breathe and I can still help someone. I can still have faith and hope, and I won't see the blessings if I'm not looking for them. Maybe the greatest blessing of all is being an example for my children and grandchildren about how to live and persevere.

Everything I thought I had lost I've found through the people who have helped me.

June 17, 2013

Joy, Strength and Survival

THE STORY OF OUR FAMILY AND TREE

*L*ast weekend was pure joy with a scoop of ice cream on top. Our two daughters and their families were both home at the same time, and you can't top that. Now that our family includes two wonderful sons-in-law and four precious grandchildren, our bonds are stronger than ever.

We all sat outside in the shade under our sprawling mulberry tree and watched the grandkids play in the sandbox and sprinkler, swim, chase bubbles and run around the backyard. We didn't even feel the 90 degree temperatures—much.

The tree's branches shade a good portion of the yard while reaching out to embrace her brood of small children, birds, squirrels, dogs, cats, and the occasional possum. It is her kingdom and she its faithful protectorate for the past 25 years.

You can lie on your back and look up through her branches at certain times of the day and her leaves are back lit by the sun against the azure canvas and radiantly outlined in white-gold. I think it might be a little bit of heaven shining through.

When our now 5-year-old grandson was just a few months old, he showed me how to see it one day. While he was lying on his back on a blanket underneath her canopy, I noticed him looking up at the leaves with something like rapture in his eyes. I lay down beside him and followed his gaze. Then I saw it, too—the radiance, through the eyes of this child.

"There are places in the world that you see with your eyes, and places that you see with your heart," Byron once said. This is one you can see with both.

We didn't always have our mulberry tree. When the girls were small we lived in Dallas—the land of short trees, concrete and freeways. An opportunity to move to Longview came along,

so we grabbed it and moved to greenness and tall, towering pines.

The house we bought was perfect for us, except for one thing—no climbing tree for our daughters, who would soon be big enough for this childhood pleasure. Growing up, I always had a climbing tree; it was my second home. Nothing sets a child's imagination free like a tree. In fact, I was mostly a squirrel during my early years.

We set out to find a suitable tree that would grow quickly. The nursery advised us that a fruitless mulberry would fit the bill, but warned the species was not especially hardy and prone to disease. Taking a chance, we bought one anyway.

Our tree grew to be beautiful—truly reflecting God's majesty and grace. Disease did not take her as predicted, but one day a 70 mph straight-line wind did.

Coming out of the blue, it whipped through the backyards of the houses on our side of the street and knocked down every tree in its path. In a matter of seconds, our tree was completely uprooted and blown to the ground.

After telling a friend about it the next day, he said, "Why don't I drive my pickup truck into your backyard, chain the tree to it, and see if I can pull it back up. Maybe it'll take root again." We had never heard such a crazy idea, frankly. "It couldn't hurt," he said.

So he came over and took down our backyard gate, drove in and chained her to the truck, then proceeded to pull her up. She lived. That was about 15 years ago. Not a "hardy species"? They need to take that part out of the description. Our tree continues to flourish and now provides shade for her grandchildren. She will be their climbing tree one day soon.

Like most families, ours has encountered a few straight line winds throughout the years. Matter of fact, one is coming through right now in the form of Alzheimer's disease. It may knock us down at times, but it won't take us out. We learned that from our tree.

Together, through God's power, our family is strong enough to stand.

But they that wait upon the Lord shall renew their strength; they shall mount up with wings as eagles; they shall run, and not be weary; they shall walk, and not faint.

—Isaiah 40:31 (KJB)

June 27, 2013

"Broke Down and Abandoned"

A few years ago, we were just outside of Fredericksburg when we I noticed this unusual sight. I wondered what the truck's sad story was. I decided to give it one, but with a happy ending.

~

As told by the truck—

I used to be shiny and powerfully built, "a very fine vehicle indeed," people would say. I helped them begin fresh lives back in the day by carrying their worldly belongings on journeys to new homes.

That was before I stopped playing by the rules.

This is what happened. I began to get bored on the drives, so to add a little excitement I began to venture onto some back roads to get to my destination. Trucks don't belong on back roads—they will tear you up.

However, I experienced such a sense of freedom and exhilaration that soon I begin to travel only back roads. It was strictly against policy, but I did not care; I was leading the life of sweet abandon.

Now, I really *am* abandoned—broke down and useless, and the weeds are slowly consuming me.

Traveling too many back roads will do that to you.

Suddenly something catches my eye. A man is coming out of the woods and walking my way. I've never even seen anyone else in this god-forsaken place. He's smiling, almost seems like he's been looking for me. But that can't be. No one would be looking for me—of that I am quite sure.

He walks up to me and runs his hand along my rusted hood. I think about how bright and shiny I used to be and suddenly, I am ashamed. He bends down and begins to pull up the weeds around me. I'm wondering why it matters to him; I am perplexed.

Then the man stands up and looks at me. "Will you let me drive you out of here?" he asks.

"Mister, I've been broke down and rusted out for a long time. I can't go anywhere," I tell him. He must be crazy. Does he think I would be hanging around here otherwise?

Instead I say, "Too many back roads. Now no one can fix me."

"I can," the man replies.

I'm really confused. Who is this man?

"I know all about you," he says. "I know the mistakes you've made and the regrets you have. I know you've given up. But I am here to say that I can make you a new creation, if you will come with me."

I am dumbfounded. How does he know all that about me? And he says he can make me new? Now that would be a miracle. Miracles don't happen...not to me, anyway.

However, the man speaks with an unexplainable authority. What if he's telling the truth? I feel a flicker of what must be hope.

Looking straight into my eyes with level gaze he asks, "Do you believe me?"

I meet his gaze for a long while, not knowing what to say. Then I realize something...I know this man. I don't know how I know him but I do. And for some reason, I trust him way down deep.

"Yes, I do believe," I answer.

He smiles and gets into my cab, then puts the key in the ignition. "Let's hit the road, Jack. I've got big plans for you."

117

As he turns the key, my engine roars to life and I drive away—a new creation.

Therefore, if anyone is in Christ, he is a new creation. The old has passed away; behold, the new has come.

—2 Corinthians 5:17 (ESV)

July 10, 2013

"Deer Moments"

GOLDEN MOMENTS IN GOD'S TIME

It was the morning after the refreshing rain earlier this week. I took the dirt path up the hill instead of continuing on the walking trail. As I got closer to the crest of the slope, I saw two deer—a buck and a doe.

Growing up a city girl, seeing deer anywhere but especially within a mile or two of my house, is always a serendipitous experience for me. They seem to possess a kind of magic, like fairies or gnomes. (I'm in the minority, I know. In East Texas, the only excitement about deer usually occurs on a deer lease.)

Later on, I had the good fortune to see four more deer when I continued down the trail, including three toddler deer, you might call them—small deer who have outgrown their spots. Sounds good to me.

Ann Voscamp (*One Thousand Gifts*) said, " To read His message in all the moments, in the waiting moments, the dark moments, the moments before blooming, I'll need to read His passion on the page; wear the lens of the Word, to read His writing in the world."

God's writing was all over the place that morning in those "deer moments." I saw His words in the night's remaining raindrops who sought refuge on the grass blades to avoid being sucked up by the parched earth. I noticed His writing within the cool breeze tickling the leaves, and the birds' and crickets' soft background music accompanying His still, small voice—the "Narrator of Creation."

Deer moments are like the gentle rain that delivers them—cleansing and refreshing for the soul, and a reminder of God's grace, provision and majesty.

I lost track of how long I stayed on top of the hill even after the two deer, who watched me curiously for a while, bounded back into the woods. I savored the multi-faceted gifts of those moments. I think deer moments must reside in God's time instead of ours— gold bricks lining the streets of His Kingdom, grains of sand on the beach of eternity.

In the deer moments, all of heaven and nature sings—even in an East Texas July.

The heavens proclaim His righteousness, and all peoples see His glory.

—Psalm 97:6 (NIV)

July 17, 2013

Alzheimer's—

A TEAM EFFORT

*I*f you've ever been to a Presbyterian church before, you've probably noticed we are a relatively staid group. In our tradition, we
joke that we like to do things "decently and in order." But—it's not
really a joke.

A few weeks ago I was sitting on the back pew at church. Since
Byron is a member of the praise team, he was up front. This particular Sunday he was also scheduled to give the children's sermon.
After the opening music and Scripture readings, Byron came down
from the choir loft to sit with the children who were gathered on
the floor. He had his music notebook because we had put the sermon in it for safekeeping the night before.

Just where that sermon was became the burning question as
he sat in front of the children who were waiting expectantly—and
tried to find it. For a few, long stretched-out minutes he flipped
through his notebook to no avail. After making a joke, he continued looking for the errant page, getting flustered. That rarely happens to Byron.

The thing is, I knew exactly where that children's sermon
was because I had put it there. So, breaking a long tradition of
Presbyterian propriety, I called out, quite loudly, from the back of
the church, "It's the blue tab."

Everyone chuckled a bit. I think they were relieved because
we've all been there and know how it feels.

The surprising thing was—I wasn't embarrassed and neither
was Byron. We were among family and it was all a moment of grace.

Byron found the page and quickly returned to his cool, collected self and replied matter-of-factly, "Oh, OK," and proceeded to give a dynamite children's sermon.

What surprised me was that several church members came up to us afterwards with tears in their eyes and told us it had been a beautiful moment—that they saw Byron and I were a team.

Yes we are, I realized. For us, this has been one of the blessings of Alzheimer's. The presence of the disease has strengthened the bonds of our marriage, like a refiner's fire.

But there are others on our team, too. We are blessed to have the unconditional love, acceptance, support and prayers of our church family as well as family and friends. They are all part of our team, as is everyone who has ever lifted us up in prayer, sent a card, made a call or stopped by to say they cared.

Teams are important. Without a team, you can't even play the game. You need help and support because no one can go it alone. Reach out to someone with Alzheimer's. Join their team. There are those who have few or none to help them make it through the dark night. Many stay out of sight and suffer in silence because of the stigma, or simply because they have ceased to matter to anyone.

You can indeed make a difference—please do.

August 16, 2013

Don't Miss the Beauty

FOR THE WEEDS

We recently returned from a "Bucket List" trip to Yellowstone National Park and the Grand Tetons—amazing and indescribable beauty to behold.

But beauty is really everywhere, isn't it? This beauty...no matter where we look. Sometimes hidden—but there, nonetheless. Beauty and blessings—one and the same. All beauty is blessing, and all blessings are beautiful.

But we have to notice, not just look. Therein lies the rub.

God has scraps of wonder hidden everywhere. Like buried treasure or Easter eggs, we have to seek to find them. Small wonders are vessels for exuberance, light and the magnificent.

I first realized this when I was 13 and like most of my friends, regularly filled with teenage angst.

One day my best friend and I were walking along a blacktop road bordered by nothing but litter and overgrown weeds. Then I happened to look up at the clouds and noticed they were glorious. Then I looked down at the weeds and saw determined blossoms pushing through the entanglement.

My spirit lightened, and I felt hope. What it conveyed to me was there is beauty even in the mess of life. To my 13-year-old mind, it was like hearing a happy secret. All was not lost. I wish I could have verbalized it to my friend but instead we just walked on, in the manner of young girls.

I did not understand it well at the time, but now I do—beauty and light are everywhere all the time because we are covered by

His grace. Grace becomes the lens through which we view life. Therefore, hope lives. I wish I could have told my friend.

Looking back, that seemingly insignificant brief moment became a defining moment in my life.

Through the lens of grace, life is loveliness—in the seemingly unbeautiful or insignificant as well as the grand and glorious. We dare not miss the forest for the trees, or the beauty for the weeds.

For the earth is saturated with the Glory of God.

You must search for the loveliness…
It is not obvious; it is scattered;
But when you find it, it touches you
And binds you to it like a great secret oath
Taken in silence.

—Struthers Burt, Jackson Hole

August 22, 2013

Leave the Margins!

*O*ur days are like pages, and pages need margins. They are less confusing and more readable and pleasing to the eye. Life isn't meant to be all page and no margins.

Our pages tend to get out of control sometimes, at least mine do. Sometimes days, weeks, months or even seasons of my life get too chaotic—crammed full and stressful, usually in part because I've forgotten to leave margins. Margins cushion us against chaos.

If you remember to live in moments, though, and not bigger units of time, you've got it nailed. Moments are too small to have room for chaos, only Kingdom. Moments are margins in themselves.

But how often do we remember?

During hectic or stressful times the writing on my page becomes overcrowded, messy and illegible. Misspelled words, faulty grammar and meaningless, superficial sentences become the norm. When my page gets filled, instead of stopping and rejuvenating, I begin to write in the margins, too. Then life quickly becomes all cluttered page and no margin, diverted from the purpose for which God intended. As Shakespeare wrote, "Life...a tale told by an idiot, full of sound and fury, signifying nothing."

When I leave the margins clean and pristine, they become a resting place for my eyes, a sigh of relief for my cluttered mind. We need a place to be still—time to listen and not do—a time for restoration. We need to leave margins so we can live out love. We need spaces in our busyness through which we can hear God.

When I get regular and sufficient rest in the margins, I write more legibly and thoughtfully. I have clarity of mind. I have room to love and to serve. And, I feel God's presence and peace.

Only then can He use me for His glory and the purpose for which He made me.

August 29, 2013

Numbering Our Days

COUNTING THE MOMENTS OF GOD'S GRACE

*D*o you have occasions when you wonder if you're hearing correctly, or at all, what God is trying to say to you through the "alphabet of our days?" The problems you encounter or the movies you watch, books you read, the raise you got or job you lost, the people He puts in your path?

Sometimes I forget to remember He is speaking to me through everything. Probably because I don't put, "Be still and listen to God," on my "to-do list" and my list is bad about taking over my real life.

Other times, however, what God says to me is crystal clear. Like when a song "coincidentally" comes on the radio and speaks directly to the state of my heart and circumstances, or a when a sermon slams the ball straight to my court.

Often, a Bible passage or verse will zing me. It might be something I have heard or read before, but this particular time it happens to show up with flashing neon lights. Then I'll maybe get in the car and hear the same theme in a praise song and I'll come home and see it posted it on Facebook. (I know what you're thinking—eventually, everything is posted on Facebook so that doesn't really count.)

Anyway, I know what all that means—I better take it to the bank.

Yesterday morning I read two verses in flashing lights—"Teach us to number our days and recognize how few they are, and help us to spend them as we should" (Psalms 90:2 TLB), and "Every morning tell Him, 'Thank you for your kindness,' and every evening rejoice in all His faithfulness" (Psalms 92:2 TLB).

I wrote them down. I always have to write down neon light-type insights in my journal so they'll find a niche in my brain and stay put.

Then I picked up my current favorite devotional book by Ann Voscamp *(One Thousand Gifts Devotional)* and happened to open it to page 125—flashing neon lights again—"The way to learn to number our days is to count the moments of His grace."

Now that's an exuberating insight. Numbering our days by counting the moments of his grace? What a life-changing, paradigm-shifting and amazing concept. It makes me not want to miss a single thing.

Voscamp continues, "Number the beats, record the blessings, enumerate the gifts, see one at the center of it all, and know there is much and it is fleeting and it is in the accounting of a life that we accumulate thanks for anything in life. This way is gone all too soon. Who keeps track to keep a heart of wisdom, to keep a perspective that keeps Him in focus?"

I think of the moments of grace I might have already missed had I not been tuned in at the right time. What if I had missed—life?

Thanks be to God for His tender mercies.

September 6, 2013

Through Pain, "Speak Life"

BE THE BLESSING

"Pain is God's megaphone," wrote C.S. Lewis in *The Problem of Pain.*

It was for us. With Alzheimer's disease, pain's volume gets turned up slowly, then you wake up one day and it's blaring and you think you can't stand it anymore.

Lewis continued, "It [pain] removes the veil and plants the flag of truth within the fortress of a rebel soul. If the first and lowest operation of pain shatters the illusion that all is well, the second shatters the illusion that what we have, whether it be good or bad in itself, is our own and enough for us."

So we learn all is not well and what we have or had is not our own and not enough—therefore our lives are shattered and we have no hope, right? That's a pretty good description of how you feel at first, anyway.

But back off, and everything looks different when viewed from God's perspective. God—"The Great Paradigm-Shifter." The weak are strong, the poor are rich, and pain—the illusion-shatterer, becomes the vessel for truth and life.

Through His grace if we allow Him, God changes our focus from how we can avoid pain to how He can use us as we walk through it. We begin to see a new purpose in life though our circumstances are still far from what we would have chosen. God begins to speak through our brokenness and give us a new calling and in effect—new lives.

The common denominator of the call is the same for all of us—in whatever circumstances we're in, we've got to "Speak Life," and Love, and Hope.

We've got to speak it with the words we say and the way we live—for we are called to *be* the blessing.

September 26, 2013

Normal is Overrated

LIFE WITH ALZHEIMER'S

*T*his photo typifies our life with Alzheimer's.
It also typifies our life before Alzheimer's.
It typifies life being married to Byron Horne.
Normal is relative, and we all know there are no normal relatives.

This sounds like the kind of random statement Byron would make in his best Groucho Marx impression. Except I just thought of it myself (I think—unless I subconsciously plagiarized it.) The point being, you know you've been married a long time when you start thinking like your spouse, especially one who sees all the world as potential joke and pun material and you don't. (I literally have a one-joke brain, but at least it is a good one.)

For almost 37 years it has been like this—spontaneous, crazy, unpredictable—a great ride, barring a few bang-ups and wrong turns. I learned long ago one thing I can count on with Byron is unpredictability, but mostly in a good way. He can also iron, which I find very handy in a husband. He can sew on buttons, as well, and also make the shirt on which to sew the buttons.

The man possesses incredible organization skills and is disgustingly neat—which is good or we would be in trouble.

It doesn't seem right or fair that all this would fit together in one person.

Before Alzheimer's, Byron had an incredible memory and was one of those people no one wanted to play "Trivial Pursuit" with. I don't see how he had room in his brain for all the obscure facts he knew. I always told him it was a shame he didn't leave room for any of the important stuff. What I didn't admit was that I had noticed the important stuff somehow found its way in, anyway.

Oh, but there's more. He has always been able to play any song he has ever heard on his guitar by ear, and he's heard them all. He can sing, draw, act, impersonate and dance (or at least fake it very well). The thing he's best known for, however, are his incredibly bad jokes and puns.

As I wrote this, it was Halloween night and Byron was sitting on the front porch swing wearing his flamingo hat and waiting for unsuspecting trick-or-treaters with whom to engage in comedic dialogue before they would receive any candy. It was a cruel trick, but it worked.

Alzheimer's has changed some things, but not all of them. It has been slow progressing so we have had time to adjust to each day's or week's "new normal."

October 31, 2013

How Not to Buy a Car

We have always bought our cars used and keep them until they approach the 200,000 mile mark. Therefore, we haven't had that much practice in the art of car-buying lately. How quickly you block it out of your mind. But we knew our gas-guzzling Trailblazer had to go after we drove a rented Sonata on vacation this summer.

We started off with it while visiting friends in Bozeman, Montana, then spent the next week exploring Yellowstone, the Grand Tetons and Jackson Hole—all on three-quarters of a tank of gas. This included a fair amount of extra driving due to my poor navigational skills, as well as being in multiple traffic jams because of buffalo crossing the road. You can't make buffalo go anywhere they don't want to go, so everyone just sits there wasting gas until they decide to get out of the road.

Why, we use three-quarters of a tank every time we drive to Forney and back to see two of our grandsons. Driving up to Denton and back to see our other two takes a full tank. At $65 to $70 a tank, that ain't cheap.

Reluctantly we steeled ourselves to re-enter the nebulous and tricky world of car-buying again. In our experience, it is like navigating between land mines. Now I do not mean to imply all car dealerships or sales people are like that, just some of the ones we have been unfortunate enough to deal with. Of course there are bad apples in every business and profession.

One day we saw an ad in the paper advertising a used Sonata at one of the major car dealerships for a good price. I Googled the business and found it had lots of good reviews, so we decided to check it out. I figured out after the fact that their employees must have written them.

We got there and told the nice salesman (aren't they all nice at first?) what we were looking for, the key words being "used cars," and that we had seen a particular car in the paper we were interested in. "Let's see if we really have it," he said (the first sign of trouble). So we all trekked through the parking lot looking for the car that may or may not have been really there.

As we were looking for the illusive car, he pointed out several others and asked if we wanted to sit in them. "Are they used?" I had to ask each time. (Car salesmen are pretty forgetful, I discovered, or else can't tell the difference between "new" and "used.") This one was the same way and, by golly, every car he pointed out was new. Finally I told him, just a *tad* more forcefully, that we wanted a used car as in u-s-e-d, and since he didn't seem to have any, we would have to leave.

Of course, he suddenly found the very car we had asked about. After much haggling (which involved the salesman going back and forth into the building to talk with his as yet unseen boss (perhaps the Great Oz?) while leaving us out in the parking lot in the hot sun, it actually got down to a price we might consider, along with our two trade-in's. (Don't ask me why we stuck around this long—I have no idea. Maybe pre-heat stroke muddled our thinking.)

The salesman then granted us an inside visit and sat us down at a table to have "the talk." After a long while (because I'm sure he had lots of important stuff to do first), the "Big Dog" himself came sauntering out, sporting a well-cut suit, shiny cuff links and gold chain, highlighted hair and overly white movie star teeth which he flashed often. The highlights made me a little wary—men who have highlights seem to me like they're trying too hard. (Hey, it's OK for women to do anything we want with our hair, because hair is our territory. Call it sexist if you want.)

"So nice to meet you," Big Dog gushed as he extended his hand. Then he ventured a totally off-the-wall question—"Do you like our music?" That was the conversation opener. Actually, I wanted to say, the music made me suspicious because it was contemporary Christian praise music. Now I love praise music, but in a place you suspect is using it to let you know what good people they are—not so much. I conceded to myself that I could be wrong and was probably too quick to jump to conclusions.

But I wasn't. My suspicions were confirmed with his next statement. "We're Christians, you know. That's why we play praise music." My warning lights doubled up their flashing.

"Oh really?" I wanted to say to him. "I'll bet it happens to be a good marketing tool, also." I just think he ought to be glad Jesus didn't stop by to buy a car that day and try that line on him. Especially if He knew how Big Dog was going to try to close the deal in the next five minutes.

"So," he said as he put his elbows on the table, folded his hands with their manicured nails and leaned toward us. Then he popped the question, "Are you ready to buy this car?"

"Not now," I firmly told him, and reminded him that we had reiterated to the salesman from the beginning that under no circumstances were we buying a car today; that anything we were interested in we would have to go home and think about first. His face suddenly morphed into a sneer, reminiscent of a bully on the playground taunting his victim—no more suave, caring demeanor.

"You mean, after all I've done for y'all, you're not going to take this deal?" he said in his most incredulous "I-can't-believe-what-I-just-heard" voice. He continued this "I can't believe it" game and was stopping just short of threatening us, sounded like. We stood up and I told him that was it—we were leaving. He suddenly changed his tactics and became placating again as we were walking out. It was way too late, and we never looked back.

Our second hunt for a used car occurred about a week later after we had recovered from our first attempt. The results were similar. We walked out of that place too, after having had two hours of our time wasted to see only two cars. (Long story, and longer wait.)

After telling a friend about our bad luck, she mentioned that we ought to try the website, www.newcars.com. It is a way to compare prices from dealerships across the area on whatever type of vehicle you're looking for. You just have to fill out a simple questionnaire, which includes your phone number and email so they can contact you.

In retrospect, I can see where it would be very helpful if you limited your search and clicked on one car to look up and maybe click only one or two of the dealerships to check out. However, it is not wise if you click on four vehicles and "all dealerships in the area."

I found that out very quickly, when the phone started ringing a few minutes after I pressed "enter." (It was 8 p.m.; they have operators standing by, apparently.) And, the website doesn't give you just dealerships in the Longview area as I had assumed, but every dealership, used and new, in East Texas including Tyler, Kilgore, Mineola and Gladewater, and a few others which I can't remember now; it is all a blur.

All this is times four cars each since I made four requests.

My cell phone has been ringing steadily for almost two weeks now. (After about the first three calls, I realized the big mistake I had made and my survival instincts kicked in. I began to ignore every call I got if I didn't recognize the number, and my voice mail box filled up. I am getting emails every day from all the salesmen who left unanswered messages on my voice mail. Now, I am beginning to get follow-up emails on all the unanswered emails.

When will I learn to think before I click?

The Trailblazer is looking so much better; we may just take out a loan for the gas.

November 8, 2013

I'm Just Byron's Wife

*W*hat the minister said 37 years ago was, "I now pronounce you man and wife," not "patient and caregiver."

Unless I'm remembering incorrectly, "caregiving" is included in the general job description of marriage, as "in sickness and in health." It's something we do, not who we are. I am still Byron's wife and he is still my husband, regardless of whether he has Alzheimer's disease or not.

Wonder when we stopped being husband and wife in the eyes of the world and got switched to our new titles? I'll tell you when—the day he was diagnosed.

Our Alzheimer's support group all dislikes the caregiver label too, just as much as our spouses hate being called "patients."

Byron kind of smirks when he hears someone ask if I'm his caregiver. I am sure he's thinking, "Yeah, right. So why am I still folding the towels and loading and unloading the dishwasher and ironing her clothes?" (I'll tell you why, dear husband—because you and I both know you are better at it than I am!)

Just the other day we were getting Byron some new CPAP machine equipment. The employee waiting on us knew Byron had Alzheimer's and asked me if I was his caregiver. Suddenly I was done with the term. I told the guy, "No, I'm not his caregiver; we're partners in this," meaning the disease.

Why didn't I just say, "No, I'm not his caregiver, I'm his wife." Wife is all-encompassing. We don't need a separate word for each thing that is part of our relationship.

You've got to start somewhere to begin changing society's perception of the disease, and this might be a good place.

November 22, 2013

Giving Thanks

FOR MY FIRST FRIEND

I was six, shy, skinny-legged and freckle-faced and had never had a friend before. I was a day-dreamy kind of child and lived mostly in my imagination because I had spent the great majority of my time in a car—not much else you can do in a car. It couldn't have been much fun to have a kid in the car with you for six years, but my father traveled, so my mother and I traveled with him.

We had never lived in just one place before, except for two 6-month stays in an apartment. My parents told me I had been to every state in America. Too bad that all I can remember is stepping on a cactus in Arizona. That, and standing up in the front seat between them, breathing cigarette smoke day after day. They kept a window cracked, thinking the smoke was going out, but mostly it didn't. However, I survived and never, ever considered smoking. So there you go.

We finally moved into a real house in Shreveport, Louisiana, when it was time for me to start first grade. I remember standing in my front yard that first day at our new house and seeing a pretty little blonde-haired girl walking underneath an umbrella across the street. I don't think it was raining.

It remains a vivid memory to this day because that little girl became my first friend. Little did we know God was putting us together as fellow sojourners and best friends throughout child-hood for the next 12 years. What a magnificent time it was to be!

My best friend was lucky because she was an only child and I had a little brother and baby sister. My mother worked and her mother stayed home. Our families both had housekeepers, not because we were rich, but because that was how it was back then. She had a television and I didn't, at least not until I was in third grade. She got to wear red Keds and my mother made me wear clunky Saddle Oxfords since they had "arch support." Other than that, we were exactly alike, except she didn't have skinny legs or freckles. And she wasn't shy. To me, she was perfect.

Every day I was knocking on her door or she was knocking on mine. "Can you play?" we would always ask.

I liked to play at my friend's house because there were no little kids, plus her mother was always making cookies and candy, painting or arranging flowers. She had been a cheerleader in high school and was very pretty and nice. She would let us watch scary movies on television, like "Thriller." My mother wouldn't let me watch scary shows so that was my big childhood "rebellion"—watching "Thriller" across the street.

My friend's yard also had the most wonderful climbing tree—a big mimosa with pink fluffy blossoms all over it that felt as soft as a kitten's fur against your cheek. The blossoms smelled like sweet bursts of joy, even better than honeysuckles, except you couldn't suck on them.

The mimosa tree also had dark crackly pods hanging on its branches in the fall, and if you peeled them open you would see little hard brown seeds in a neat row. We would pick them out and pretend to eat them when we played "Squirrels," which was our most frequent tree game.

When we weren't in the mimosa tree, we would do all manner of things—pretend we were the "Lennon Sisters," dig in the dirt with the good kitchen spoons, ride bikes with no hands or pretend to be orphans. It felt good not having any parents to mind, we decided.

Dolls were a big favorite with us—baby dolls at first and then Barbie dolls. We were part of the original Barbie doll generation. My friend had a Barbie, Ken and Midge dolls, and I had a Barbie and an Allen doll—(I'm not sure why; maybe Allen was cheaper than Ken.) The Barbie clan soon became like the genealogy chapters in the Old Testament—you couldn't keep up with all the names, characters, spin-offs and knock-offs.

My friend also had a Barbie house, furniture and car and we would spend hours setting it all up and dressing our Barbie's in various outfits. Soon after we got it all set up, we got tired of it and would take it all down. That was the main fun of playing Barbie dolls—the setting-up. In hindsight, it was good preparation for life—"enjoying the journey."

Another favorite pastime of ours was playing games like kickball, army or chase with the neighborhood boys about our age, along with several of the younger children on occasion. We would tolerate each other long enough to play games that required more than two people. After a while, inevitably, there were shouts of "Not fair," or "You cheated," and we would all run off our separate ways until the next time we needed teammates.

It was a good childhood—better because my friend was in it. In fact, I can't imagine what it would have been without her. Those were our "Camelot years," before the end of the innocence we all face at some point.

My friend and I saw less of each other after high school graduation and college for a while, but reconnected later on. Now, over 50 years later, she still remains one of my very best friends (although we couldn't possibly be that old).

My friend has been one of God's greatest blessings to me, and I thank Him that he put us together in that most precious time of times.

November 29, 2013

"The Last Dance"

We get to church early on Sundays since Byron has praise team rehearsal. I like to park under the tall trees and sit in the car for the next hour, just being quiet and still. On a sunny Sunday a few weeks ago, the breeze and the leaves had their game on, and I found myself drawn into their dance—a serendipitous sermon beside the parking lot.

I watched the last of the autumn leaves
skydive from their trees
and race sideways across the grass,
not touching down.
"Just a few more minutes, Papa,"
I thought I heard them say.

Skipping, rolling, swirling and running,
like children on the playground;
I could almost hear them
squealing with delight.
The end of life—
replicating the beginning.

The wind gives the leaves
a dizzying joy-ride
for their last big hurrah;
they will not go quietly
into that silent night.
No, wearing their brilliant garb
they will dance exuberantly
into the Kingdom.

May all of God's children
enter the Kingdom dancing,
skipping, rolling, swirling, and running
since the confines of the body are no more
and the soul is loosed—Oh glorious day!

You will go out in joy
and be led forth in peace;
the mountains and hills
will burst into song before you,
and all the trees of the field
will clap their hands.

—Isaiah 55:12 (ESV)

December 12, 2013

"Holding Heaven's Child"

It happened when I recently heard the MercyMe version of "Little Drummer Boy." When they came to the part, "Then He smiled at me," all of a sudden I started crying. It's like it was the first time I ever heard it. My daughter came in and said, "Mom, what's wrong?" I struggled to get the words out—"The baby Jesus just smiled at the drummer boy."

She just looked at me with that, "Oh, mom," expression, probably wondering how she turned out so normal. But—you don't have a baby smile around a grandmother, even if it's only in a song, without creating an emotional response. Especially if the baby happens to be Jesus and you hope you are playing your best for Him.

I wish I had been there, Jesus.
I would have snuggled you in my arms,
and held your fuzzy head against my cheek.
I would have stroked your satin skin,
and wiggled your little toes.
I would have kissed the back
of your sweet baby neck.

I would have looked into your eyes and smiled,
and told you how much I loved you.
And you would have smiled back at me
and lit up my soul.
I would have rocked you and sung,
"You are my Sunshine"
until you fell fast asleep.
I would have always kept you safe.
Never would I have let you go.

You grew up to be my Savior, Jesus—
the One who loves me the most
in all the world.
You snuggle me in your arms
when I am afraid,
and even when I'm not.
You look at me and smile,
and tell me how much You love me.
You light up my soul.
You rock me and sing me lullabies
during the dark nights,
and walk with me
through all my days.
I know that never will You let me go.

You breathed life into me
and gifted me with a plan,
a purpose, and gifts
to use for Your glory.
It's only because of You,
and for You—
that I live.
For you, Jesus, are my Son-Shine.

December 18, 2013

Grabbing Life

IN THE NEW YEAR

*A*ngus, our 3-year-old schnauzer, loves for us to chase him around the house. He loves it because he knows we can't catch him, and he delights in feeling superior to us. He'll leap over the couch, slide down the slick hallway going full speed, then double back and run through our legs. I think Angus fancies himself to be Superdog.

When he finally gets tired out, he will come and sit quietly on the couch beside us for a while. But you never know when he'll get up and take off again. Angus is a slippery fellow, and it is a grand moment on those rare occasions when one of us catches him. When that happens, I feel a ridiculous sense of delight and accomplishment.

Angus reminds me of my life. It also likes to race by me and run around in circles like an untrained puppy, me grabbing at it futilely. It just laughs because it knows I'll give up before long.

However, the other day I actually reached out and grabbed Life by the tail as it tried to run by. I think it was shocked. I haven't caught it in ages, and it must have thought that it had gotten the best of me.

Well, think again, Life.

My New Year's Resolution is not to let you go again. Yes, you heard me right. Don't forget you belong to me, not vice-versa, and I don't want to spend this next year chasing you around again. First thing I'm going to do, Life, is leash-train you and that includes you not trying to pull me along or stop at every bush. You are going to know who is boss and learn to sit and stay and come when you're called, by golly. No more carefree rambunctiousness and thinking the world is your rawhide.

However, as much as you get on my nerves at times, Life, I know I need to treat you with compassion and care since you're the only one I've got. Don't worry, you'll have a roof over your head and food to eat, except no more Blue Bell ice cream. That's part of the new deal—self-control. Yes, you heard me right, and yes—I know you've been through a lot. And I am not falling for it again.

Just work with me, Life, OK? And Happy New Year.

Many, O Lord my God, are the wonders You have done. The things You planned for us no one can recount to You; were I to speak and tell of them, they would be too many to declare.

—Psalms 40:5 (NIV)

January 2, 2014

The Secret

TO DOING THE IMPOSSIBLE

I'm a New Year's Resolution's nerd from way back.

Our extended family always got together at my aunt's house on New Year's Day, and everyone would be inside watching football but me. I was the one outside writing resolutions in my diary. Some years I even made checklists to go with them; maybe it was just the future first grade teacher surfacing. Anyway, I don't do that anymore. Now my resolutions go on a whiteboard—easier to erase.

One of our family traditions when our daughters were growing up was to write down our resolutions on New Year's Day (Mom's orders) and read them aloud to each other at the dinner table. I was the only one with any enthusiasm for this, but they all grudgingly went along. I saved each year's resolutions to read aloud the next year, too. We always got a good laugh out of that. (Then I retained them for future blackmail purposes.) Nowadays, it feels different facing a New Year from the viewpoint of Alzheimer's, since we are looking at a large block of time instead of moments. Time is not Alzheimer's friend. Thinking about the future is mostly not enjoyable.

So where's the hope? How much longer will there be any joy in our lives? Can we do it? Can *I* do it?

These are the middle-of-the-night thoughts that come when my defenses are down and my negativity and anxiety are up.

I have found that many times through writing, God gives me comfort and leads me to more understanding of whatever the problem or question is. There is something about objectifying thoughts and feelings by putting them on paper. Then through prayer and the writing process, God answers and encourages. Maybe not immediately, but eventually.

So I had been journaling about these thoughts and worries for a few days, seeking guidance.

The answer to, "Can I do it?" came during a half-awake time during the night about a week ago, when I must have been still "writing" in my head after a discouraging day.

A random thought was floating around in my brain about Paul being in jail but still rejoicing. Then something else Paul said came to mind that explained how he could do the "impossible."

"Not that I was ever in need, for I have learned how to get along happily whether I have much or little. I know how to live on almost nothing or with everything. I have learned the secret of contentment in every situation, whether it be a full stomach or hunger, plenty or want; for I can do everything God asks me to with the help of Christ who gives me the strength and power" (Philippians 4:11-13 TLB).

If Paul could rejoice in jail through Christ's power—then I can rejoice in Alzheimer's.

I was reassured, once again, that I was not bound, nor would I ever be, by my circumstances.

That passage is my "joy key."

Thanks be to God for his tender mercies!

January 9, 2014

Safe in His Arms

I don't like "it."

We all have an "it" in our lives at various times—a hurt, an illness, a hardship, a tragedy.

Since Byron was diagnosed in November of 2011, we have been sharing our story with the prayer that God will use our humble words to encourage others and draw them to Him. I usually write a column *after* God has brought me through a painful or discouraging time instead of in the midst of it, because I want to share His provision and hope. On the other hand, I also want to be honest about our struggles because we all have them.

For us, sometimes living with Alzheimer's is like living "Alice in Wonderland" in 3D—everything is off-kilter and skewed. Other times it is like being in the mirror house at the state fair and experiencing that almost swallowed-up, panicky feeling I used to get when I wondered if I would ever emerge again.

Thinking about entering the New Year is hard for me. I don't want to think about time moving forward. Time is not Alzheimer's friend, and I wish the clock would stop.

I tend to succumb to the Alzheimer's is a "living hell" notion when I get stressed and overwhelmed. Or, selfishly, when I just get plain tired of dealing with it and wish our lives could go back to how they were. In retrospect, life looks much easier than I remember. Why were we not more grateful?

A recent epiphany brought comfort to me and perhaps it will to some of you. I was getting close to falling into the, "where's-the light-and-maybe-I-really-am-entering-hell," mode of thinking when God shot one of those "insight arrows" my way. They serve to clear the chaos out of your mind so you can hear Him again.

The message was simple, yet earth-shattering: No matter how bad or devastating the "it" is by earthly standards, "it" can never, ever be hell. Hell is the absence of God, and God promises to be present with His people.

If the opposite of hell is being in God's presence, then not only can we endure, we can rejoice. In Christ we are safe, no matter what happens to us or our loved ones in this life. "The worst that can happen" can't even touch us or our loved ones if we are His. The body can be destroyed, but never the soul.

"The worst that can happen"—should it happen—also does not define, diminish or negate a life because our lives are not about what happens *to* us, either good or bad. They are about what happens *through* us.

Death is not a period, but simply a comma between this life and the Kingdom. No way is it a period.

Our story will continue. "What's lost is nothing to what's found, and all the death that ever was, set next to life, would scarcely fill a cup" (Frederick Buechner, *Listening to Your Life*).

He is the I AM in our story. In His arms, we will always be safe.

For I am persuaded that neither death nor life, nor angels or principalities, nor things present nor things to come, nor height nor depth, nor any other created thing, shall be able to separate us from the love of God which is in Christ Jesus our Lord.

—Romans 8:38, 39 (NKJV)

December 16, 2013

Someday Never Comes

*W*e celebrated our 37th anniversary last week. I cooked break-fast (something I don't usually do since we are cereal eaters, plus I am lazy) and on a whim got out the china, crystal and silver I always planned to use more often "someday."

The bad thing was I couldn't even remember when I had last used it—yet another good intention left undone and another layer of regret. To help alleviate it I dug our cloth napkins and good place mats out because it finally dawned on me—this "someday" I've been planning on will never come. Not unless I make it "this day."

After 37 years I have to ask myself, *why haven't we been doing this on a regular basis? Why have we not chosen to use our best for each day instead of waiting for the 'special occasion'? Why are we not living to the utmost this life we have been given?*

It occurred to me that I don't even use my "best self" every day. I usually keep her in the closet until I go somewhere. Then I bring her out, like a special party dress. When I get back home, I hang her up again and close the door. She needs her space, after all, because it's all about her. My best self is definitely a diva, and only likes to come out when it's convenient.

Since it is still January, it's legal to add a few more resolutions. Therefore, I've decided I am going to bring my best self out of the closet; she can kick and scream all she wants. I'm also going to give away our "everyday" dishes and wash our china in the dishwasher instead of being afraid it will break. What freedom there is in that thought after all these years.

Settling for second best in anything is a waste of time and sometimes money. You would not do that with a husband, or even a purse. The excuse of the best being "too much trouble" just isn't good enough when life is short and precious.

Thirty-seven years is a long time to routinely come up with excuses to not do my best. But not as long as 38.

Regret is redeemable, thanks be to God.

Someday never comes; but then again, it never existed in the first place.

This is the day that the Lord has made; let us rejoice and be glad in it.

—Psalm 118:24 (ESV)

January 22, 2014

The Blessing Tree

*O*ur Christmas tree is still up in the den, but only since it has been re-purposed to a higher calling. (Does it really matter that the initial reason for the re-purposing was not to have to climb up in the attic again?)

Its vocation is now "Blessing Tree." And it gets to keep its lights. Instead of ornaments, though, our tree is the habitat for hangable household objects that denote special blessings in our lives. Colorful note cards, now purposed for the noting of blessings, dangle from their ribbons, waiting for us to write on them. The tree has bestowed the homey aura of a first grade classroom in our den.

All to say, it's a pretty upbeat room and dares us to think sullen thoughts within its walls.

No more excuses for negativism or grumbling about what we wish were different, not in that room, anyway. I read something recently about a simple but very effective way to remember how God has graced you on the days you can't find much for which to be thankful. Just subtract—try to envision your life without certain people or things.

Shift the paradigm a bit and everything changes.

Simply saying or writing words of thanks to God can begin the change. Something like, "God, thank you for your goodness and blessings in and through Alzheimer's." Even if I'm not sure I mean it yet, saying it out loud or writing it down starts the shift.

Contrary to popular opinion, there really are blessings and opportunities in the midst of Alzheimer's, or anything for that matter. Life is pared down to the essentials during trials—the larger the trial, the more pared down it becomes. There is joy and peace in the paring of the fluff. Nothing really worthwhile comes from fluff, anyway—it is a spoiling of the spirit.

More importantly, in trials there are multiple opportunities to show God's grace through whatever situation we find ourselves in: to stay the course, to persevere, to trust, to have faith, to be thankful, to love, to be light and to finish well.

Of course these same opportunities await us all every day—you do not have to have a disease or hardship to access them. I don't tend to think about them, though, until I'm wandering in the desert.

It's easy to miss the meaning of life when everything is going your way.

Since Alzheimer's, Byron and I are both more laid-back (generally) and accepting of each other and life itself. We are living out our marriage vows and that in itself is a source of joy and strength. We have each other, our precious family, friends and so much more—not everything we want but everything we need.

Surrounding and enveloping us is the "peace that passes all understanding" that guards our hearts and minds. It is such a blessing not to have to understand everything to be content but rest in the knowledge that God is in control.

Being in the "Refiner's Fire" is not a bad thing—in fact, it is a necessary thing in order to become what God is calling us to be.

Our "Blessing Tree" will serve as a reminder of the Source of our peace whenever we feel the flames.

I have fought the good fight, I have finished the race, I have kept the faith.

—2 Timothy 4:7 (NRSV)

January 31, 2014

Please Sir,

MAY I HAVE SOME HEAT?

(Written during an icy cold snap a few weeks ago...)

*I*t's not fair. Us "rule-followers" always seem to be the ones to bring trouble upon ourselves through our best intentions.

As I write this, it is like 15 degrees or something, and I'm not talking outside. I was sitting in it right there at our kitchen table. Even the water struggled to come out of the faucet this morning, spurting and snorting, before finally making its way through what sounded like ice in the pipes.

That's because the gas man turned off our gas and took our meter away Monday evening—right before the cold front moved in. Couldn't have asked for better timing.

It is now Thursday and the gas man hasn't been back—four days and three nights of heat-stripped temperatures in our house. Luckily, a friend was able to loan us two space heaters: one for us and one for our dog and cat. Walmart, Lowe's and Home Depot were out (they all said heaters are a "seasonal" item and they don't stock them right now. Go figure.)

Our saga began quite innocuously—I happened to catch a teeny little whiff of gas around the key valve next to the fireplace that we use to turn on the gas to the pilot light. So, being a rule-follower, I called the gas company (...isn't that what they always say? *If you smell gas, call the gas company immediately).*

I never once heard, *"You should call your plumber first if you don't want to get your meter pulled."* But since this no-heat episode has been

157

underway, that is what everybody and their mother has told me. Am I the only one who hasn't heard this rule? Or maybe it's not a rule, but an "aside" from the rule—the part you should really pay attention to. This would explain why I, as a rule-follower, did not know about it.

Anyway, the operator told me since a gas leak is considered an emergency, someone would be out immediately. About two hours later, the gas man showed up; I could tell he was really worried about our "emergency."

"Too bad you didn't call the plumber first," he said, first thing. "You do have a leak, so I have to turn off your gas and take your meter to a secret hiding place so you won't sneak out, turn it back on and blow yourself up." (He didn't really say that, but I inferred that is what he meant. Why else would he take it?)

This had the makings of a bad James Bond movie.

"So we get the meter back after the plumber fixes the leak?" I asked.

"Well, no," he said. "The plumber can't just fix the leak, he has to test your gas line to see if there are any more leaks and also replace the pipes in the attic if they are made of copper and not up to the current code." (Since our house was built in the mid-'70s, we were toast.)

But that's not all. "And, to fix that leak," the gas man continued, "you're probably going to have to get a brick man to tear into that fireplace first and take the valve line out." This guy was full of good news.

"All that before we get to have our gas turned back on?" I asked, starting to feel just the slightest bit panicked. Seriously, is this real life? *My* real life?

"Yes, ma'am," he replied. I was not believing my ears. Our upcoming vacation was evaporating before my eyes (but that's OK, we probably would be frozen by then, anyway).

"But," I told him, "we only use the fireplace about twice a year—can't you just cover the whole thing up and we'll pretend it never existed?" I mean, politicians do this kind of thing all the time, and they're not even cold.

"Nope, now that I seen it, you gotta fix it." I know—before the gas meter can come back home.

By this time it was after 5 p.m. and the temperatures were heading down since the front was arriving. The gas man took his leave and our gas meter.

Actually, I don't blame him. After all, we do live in a part of Texas prone to rednecks and big talk. "A little explosion never hurt anyone, Ethel. Go hook that blasted thing back up and make me some heat, woman."

So, following the gas man's pronouncement of impending doom, I called several plumbers. The one we usually use was booked up the next day. "Too bad you didn't call me before you called the gas man," he said. "That valve probably just needed tightening." I really didn't want to hear that.

The second plumber I called was also booked up; the third one wasn't, and said he could "probably make it" by late afternoon on Tuesday.

Sure enough, the plumber showed up Tuesday about 4 p.m., and confirmed what the gas man said about tearing out the bricks and replacing the pipes in the attic. He informed us it would probably cost about $4,000. I also asked him about capping off the whole thing and not doing repairs. He said he could, but only if he didn't find any more leaks in the line.

He didn't (thank you, God), so he ended up capping it. ($4,000 still in the bank; vacation still on at this point.) Then he dismantled our water heater (this all seems so strange to me—still in the James Bond movie) and promised he would reconnect it if the inspector OK'd everything he had done.

"So do you think the inspector can come first thing in the morning?" I asked.

"No," he said. "The inspector probably won't make it at all, tomorrow, since first I need to put this repair on file at City Hall. Then the inspector has to pick it up before he can come out. So if he doesn't get it tomorrow morning, it'll be the next day (Thursday) before he comes." These people live very complicated lives.

Well, apparently the inspector did not get it soon enough because he didn't come yesterday.

In the four days since our heat was cut off, the temperature has been steadily dropping and our meter is still off having fun at wherever meters go when they're off duty. I'm sure it's probably sitting at a bar with the other confiscated meters, toasting to their good fortune and time off, and laughing about the sad plight of their people. "Yep, *now* they'll appreciate us," they are telling each other.

And in the meantime, we are still cold, very cold. The dog and the cat don't understand that "inside" now feels like "outside." They are very confused and will probably develop trust issues.

I am sure you're wondering by now, "Why don't they all just go somewhere that has heat and hang out?" Well, I'll tell you why—it's because we have to stay home and wait for everyone to show up, because if they come and we're not there—we are back to "go" and start over, without heat. And not one of 'em can *ever* tell us what time they're coming, or if they're positively absolutely sure they'll really "make it" on any given day.

Before we get our heat back on today as promised, hopefully, three things have to happen, and in this exact order:

1. The inspector has to show up to see if the plumber made any mistakes.
2. Then the plumber has to come back and hook our hot water heater back up.
3. Finally, the gas man has to come back, light our hot water heater and put our meter back.

Sounds like the definition of "bureaucracy," and we all know how that works.

Footnote: The inspector came out and our heat turned back on at the end of the fourth day so, $400 later, we were finally warm again.

February 6, 2014

Shattered Dreams

A PRELUDE TO JOY?

*I*t was a wonderful, throw-back kind of time. We were at an engagement party last weekend, and around lots of friends we hadn't seen in a while, along with many people we didn't know. These big group kinds of things are usually hard for Byron, since his Alzheimer's makes it difficult for him to follow more than one strand of conversation. That's why he is usually quiet unless he's conversing one-on-one.

But last Saturday night, I watched him talking and laughing with groups of friends like I haven't seen him do in a long time—relaxed, happy and being himself, just like the old days. I don't know what the normalizing "X" factor was that night, but I was thankful. My heart was light seeing him enjoy himself so much. I imagined how good it must have made him feel to "fit in" again.

It is nice to have those occasional reprieves. Because the reality is, Byron is painfully aware changes are occurring and sometimes it terrifies him that he cannot stop the insidious thief inside his brain.

People will ask him how he's doing and he will say fine, because mostly he is.

Sometimes he's not, though, because Alzheimer's is a demon that never lets go.

But do you know what? He is still thankful for so many things in his life. That is just one more reason I love this man and stand in awe of him. Alzheimer's does not stop him from thanking God for his many blessings every single day, multiple times. You would think he was one of the most blessed men on earth to hear him pray.

Well, just maybe he is? When you're talking about God's realm, I wouldn't be surprised by anything since it is all topsy-turvy of what the world calls "truth."

"Shattered dreams are a prelude to joy," wrote Larry Crabb (*Shattered Dreams: God's Unexpected Path to Joy*). I'm not saying I like it, but I'll put my money on it.

Shattered dreams mold us into God-seekers. And God-seekers are joy-finders.

You will seek me and find me, when you seek me with all your heart.

—Jeremiah 29:13 (ESV)

February 14, 2014

Living with Alzheimer's

Figuratively speaking, from a family member's point of view...

You get up, ready to start your day—energetic and enthusiastic. You come into the kitchen and discover the coffee pot will not work.

And you can't fix it.

A few days later you try to iron something, but the iron won't heat up.

And you can't fix it.

The day after that, the light bulbs burn out in several rooms all at the same time. You put new ones in but nothing happens.

And you can't fix it.

You start to wonder, *What the heck?* You begin to feel anxious each morning when you wake up, wondering what won't work next.

A few days go by and nothing else breaks. *Whew*, you think. Glad things seem to be getting back to normal. You relax a bit.

The next day you get up and go into the kitchen, and discover the refrigerator and the stove are broken.

And you can't fix them.

You finally realize that eventually, every single thing in your house is going to break and you are not going to be able to fix one single thing.

But since you can't fix it, fixing is not the point, apparently.

There is something else you're supposed to do...

Maybe show grace in the brokenness?

Maybe trust and give thanks in the brokenness?

In the whole broken, unfathomable, unfixable mess—maybe you show grace, trust and give thanks?

After all, God is there in the brokenness.

I think that might be the point.

I will praise you, O Lord,
with all my heart;
I will tell of your wonders.
I will rejoice and be glad in you.
I will sing praise to your name,
O Most High.

—Psalms 9:1,2 (NIV)

February 21, 2014

How Then Should We Live?

I love a list, and am never without one. I'll make up stuff to do, just so I can have a list. Lists are so logical, and I am not. They instill in me a sense of order.

I recently reread a favorite familiar Bible passage, Philippians 4, and something occurred to me. It sounded suspiciously like a list disguised as a paragraph. I decided to take a few liberties and write it as a list and sure enough, it has the makings of an excellent one. The logic comes through as well as the grace.

Magazines have missed this wonderful opportunity for a "Ten How-To" points article as far as I know. Here it is, loosely translated:

1. Always be full of my joy—it's yours.
2. Don't worry about anything—just pray. Tell me your needs and wants.
3. Thank me for my answers even *before* I give them.
4. As you do this, you will experience My peace, which is too wonderful for your mind to understand.
5. My peace will then keep your mind and heart quiet and at rest as you continue to trust in Me.
6. Fix your mind on what is noble, pure, lovely, admirable, excellent, right and praiseworthy. (A list within a list!) Then you will have no room for negative thoughts.
7. Think about all you can praise Me for and be glad about.
8. Put into practice all you have learned. (Use it or lose it.)
9. Learn to be content in every situation. Be happy whether you have much or little.
10. Then the God of peace will be with you.

This is a list that needs to be written not on paper or a whiteboard, but on our heart.

Rejoice in the Lord always. I will say it again: Rejoice! Let your gentleness be evident to all. The Lord is near. Do not be anxious about anything, but in every situation, by prayer and petition, with thanksgiving, present your requests to God. And the peace of God, which transcends all understanding, will guard your hearts and your minds in Christ Jesus.

Finally, brothers and sisters, whatever is true, whatever is noble, whatever is right, whatever is pure, whatever is lovely, whatever is admirable—if anything is excellent or praiseworthy—think about such things. Whatever you have learned or received or heard from me, or seen in me—put it into practice. And the God of peace will be with you.

—Philippians 4:4-9 (NIV)

March 8, 2014

Talking About Alzheimer's—

GETTING RID OF THE ELEPHANT!

*I*t was a lolling, lazy kind of Saturday afternoon a few weeks ago—a relaxing day of visiting with our daughters and watching the little boy cousins play and otherwise try to tear the house apart, like little boys are prone to do. After lunch the twins went down for their naps and 3-year-old Karl sat quietly in his mother's lap, sucking his thumb and holding out for more time.

It dawned on me the room was almost kid-less, or as close as it was going to get, anyway. I realized this was the chance we had been waiting for to talk with Amanda and Karly sans distractions. I knew I'd better jump on it, and quickly.

This was the deal: Our counselor suggested that we have another face-to-face and in-depth conversation with our daughters about Byron's Alzheimer's with everyone present, since it had been awhile. The goal was that talking about it together would continue to build openness and strength, as well as giving us an opportunity to encourage each other as we listened and shared our concerns and fears.

Well, talking about Alzheimer's is not our favorite thing. It can be a little unnerving. Plus, good luck getting everyone to agree to doing it. It's hard to bring Alzheimer's to center stage; it is much easier if it's tucked over in a corner. Admittedly though, sometimes the disease's uninvited and unacknowledged presence flits and buzzes around the tops of our conversations like a bothersome fly. I would just as soon swat it.

Byron and I agreed we had to spring it on our daughters when they had nowhere to run. Then we would be doing our part to keep the proverbial elephant out of the room.

I waited nervously for my chance. Finally, there was a lull in the conversation and I grabbed it. "Hey, do y'all want to talk about Alzheimer's?" I asked casually, like I was asking about a favorite movie and not this huge thing that had dropped on our family like a boulder, forever altering the course of our lives. (*Altering*, not shattering. With Christ, you don't shatter, or rather—*He* does not shatter.)

Everything stopped, and I caught three distinct "deer-in-the-headlight" expressions. (I had only expected two, and suddenly I realized I was in this alone. Just great; I love being the sole instigator of unpleasant discussions.)

Recklessly, I plunged ahead; there was no turning back now. "I think while we are all together it'd be a good thing to talk about." They just stared at me—like, "Why?" I was about to tell them the counselor made me do it and bail when Karly spoke up. The question she asked had been on her mind awhile, I could tell. I breathed a sigh of relief, because now I knew "the talk" was exactly what we needed to do.

During the ensuing discussion we talked about some things that had been tiptoed around before, like how Byron's Alzheimer's might look further down the road. We encouraged each other and shed a few tears. Byron reaffirmed to his daughters that he was good with his life and having Alzheimer's. "It's something I've had to accept and live with, and just go on," he said. "After all, I've got you all and the grandsons and good friends—so many blessings." That same courageous attitude he's had all along—what a legacy to pass on to them.

Afterwards, we joined hands and prayed. Our daughters prayed the most beautiful prayers that struck to the core of my heart and still make me cry to think about them. That our grown children have matured in the faith and know God intimately and trust in Him is my deepest joy. I know they will be OK as we continue to walk through this valley; in fact, I know they will always be OK, no matter what. That is the best thing a parent can know.

I was reassured that our family, through God's strength, is rock-solid.

Alzheimer's cannot destroy us. To the contrary, we will continue to praise Him in the midst of it.

March 27, 2014

Living on a Lark

To affect the quality of the day, that is the highest of the arts.

—Henry David Thoreau

⟋‿⟍

*I*t turned into a carefree lark—a freeing, dance-to-the-music kind of day, although it didn't start out that way.

Byron had been scheduled to have a gig on a recent Saturday— the "walk around" kind where he works the crowd with his trademark brand of wit and silliness.

His persona for the day was that of a leprechaun, complete with green outfit, top hat, pointed ears and Irish brogue. At the last minute he also added a red clown nose. (You don't ask creative people "Why?")

We showed up at the appointed time, but the event had closed early. What to do when you're all dressed up and nowhere to go? A leprechaun can't just go home, particularly one with a red nose. It's just not right.

We decided to visit our drugstore, Louis Morgan No. 4. It's a stop we usually make anyway when Byron is in costume. Going to Louis Morgan is a social event in itself. We can see everybody in town if we hang out there half an hour. The employees are fun people and our pharmacist, in particular, gets a kick out of seeing Byron's various personae.

Not surprisingly, he was a hit.

But where next? Byron was just getting wound up. "Let's go get some yogurt," I suggested.

Because it was a beautiful, sunny day the store was packed with children and their parents. When the leprechaun walked in, everyone smiled and the fun began.

That's his gift, to be able to light up a room. Byron can do it even when he's not in costume. It is his "greatness."

I recently read a wonderful book called *Creating Moments of Joy,* by Jolene Brackey. I recommend it to anyone who has a family member or friend with Alzheimer's. Brackey talks about "remembering a person's greatness" in order to bring joy to that individual.

To know what their greatness is, she said, think about what gift or talent brought them great joy throughout their lives. Then, ask them about it and in doing so, you will give it back to them.

Byron, witty and joking in his authentic-sounding Irish brogue, was living his greatness and at the top of his game as he subtly worked the room and made the children giggle.

Suddenly, I got it. For Byron, life itself is one big gig opportunity he can tap into anytime and anywhere, be it the drugstore or a yogurt place or walking down the street. There are plenty of opportunities to use his gifts of humor and entertaining—his "greatness." We don't have to wait until someone books him.

One of his deepest desires is to feel he still has meaning and purpose. We all feel that way sometimes, but people with Alzheimer's have a particularly hard time with it.

All I'll need to say to Byron on any given day is, "Hey, who do you want to be today?" Then we'll hit the streets and shops.

The question is, why didn't this occur to me sooner?

Byron can be Santa in July, the Easter Bunny in January and wear a red nose with every costume if he so desires. It doesn't matter who or what or where he is. What matters is the laughter and joy he can bring to others, and the fulfillment and pleasure he will receive in return.

So if you ever see us roaming around town with Byron wearing a gorilla mask (he has one) or something, you'll know what we're up to—on a lark, celebrating his greatness. I don't ever want him to forget it.

I won't—I don't think anyone will.

April 3, 2014

Something Beautiful

THROUGH ALZHEIMER'S

Some days when I look around me, all I can see are remnants of our used-to-be lives.

That's when I start to hear the darkness sniff around the crack under the door, always quick to recognize a potential opportunity to slip in.

As the disease slowly changes our world, I remind myself—life is change. And Jesus did warn us not to become attached to the things of this world. But that's hard to do when they're your things and your plans and your lives and you are indeed, attached.

I protest—I'm not ready for dust in the wind. I just want us to have lots more of...I don't know, our attachments, I guess. Nothing fancy, though. Just the simple things, like playing with the grandsons, dancing, laughing...please, God.

"I don't know if I can do this," I think to myself, again. I pray and cry and complain to Him.

Then our twin grandsons come to visit. There is nothing like grandsons to knock out negativity. I remember again that "moment" is key—live in the joy of the moment. God can especially use silly little boys to accomplish this purpose, because they possess the particular gift of moments.

After they left, we sat out under our big backyard tree at dusk and had a glass of wine while finishing off the twins' leftover vanilla wafers. A mockingbird and a frog, or maybe a cricket, had a duet going. In the reverberating stillness, we listened to creation wind down for the night.

I asked Byron how he was feeling. "Peaceful," he said, "because you're sitting here with me."

The powerful gift of presence—I forget sometimes. God's presence with us, our presence with each other. It is how we will make it.

I'll never know why God allowed the Alzheimer's, but I do know He is walking with us through it. Even the times I can't sense His presence, I know He's there.

I also sense He is making something new through Byron's disease that is touching others. Something is being taken away, but more importantly, something is being given.

Through this trial, we can allow ourselves to become despairing and bitter—we've all been there. Or, we can have faith and point to Him as the source of our hope and allow His Light to shine through us. May God give me the strength to do this.

Then our trial becomes something beautiful and new—a gift to someone else, for His glory.

April 24, 2014

"Illuminated by Grace"

In the morning
I step into the backyard
and become immersed
in the familiar, soothing greenness
of God's ever-renewing creation.

A light breeze
carries on its wings
the melody of chimes
and birdsong.
The day's virgin light
filters through the leaves above,
transforming them
into brilliant diamonds,
as His light transforms us.

Nature's metaphors
for His love and joy abound—
woven into the fabric
of each new day,
illuminating us
with His grace.

I sit, soaking in His presence,
praying for His perspective
and delighting in His Glory.
He whispers to me,
"Remember, child—
My joy
is your strength."

My heart overflows
and I thank God
for His tender mercies
and loving-kindness
which begin anew each day.

This is the day the Lord has made; let us rejoice and be glad in it.

—Psalm 118:24 (ESV)

May 8, 2014

Grace Like Rain

Recently I came across this quote by a person with Alzheimer's: "When you have Alzheimer's you gain a super power—the power to become invisible in a room full of people. Everyone talks over you, around you and about you but never to you. Once you say the magic words, 'I've got Alzheimer's'—you disappear."

This observation is only slightly exaggerated, and a sad commentary on how our society views the disease.

Like most people with Alzheimer's, Byron struggles with occasional feelings of "not mattering" anymore. When you know you are losing yourself you cannot help but question when those particular qualities that make you a unique, worthwhile individual will be gone. You wonder if perhaps you are viewed as an engine in the process of being stripped-down because occasionally, that is how you view yourself.

On a recent Sunday in church, Byron was reassured in a poignant, compelling way that he still matters and has gifts to offer.

It was our first time to do the children's chat together since we are now working as a team. Afterwards, the pastor expressed her appreciation to Byron for his longtime children's ministry, as well as his music ministry and general *joie de vivre*. She also thanked him for the courageous ways he has shared his journey with his church family and the Longview community from the beginning.

Then a surprising thing happened. The congregation began applauding and soon, everyone was on their feet. It touched both of us to the core and brought tears to our eyes. Through the love of our church, the strong arms of Christ embraced us and His "grace like rain" fell down, bringing sustenance to our souls.

We are blessed by so many who reach out and support us in myriad ways—prayers, kind words, hugs, notes and phone calls.

(Byron is also blessed by people who will listen to his corny jokes and puns.)

It is all grace, and we are very appreciative and thankful. Through each of you, God continues to encourage us.

It is my prayer that every person and family who suffers from this soul-wrenching disease will have such support and affirmation.

I thank my God every time I remember you.

—Philippians 1:3 (NIV)

May 21, 2014

Joy, Grief and "Bentley Beaver"

$\mathcal{M}$y own children, along with my first and second-graders, found out early on the children's picture book, *The Story of Bentley Beaver*, by Marjorie Weinman Sharmat, would make me cry—every time. Never let children discover your weaknesses, because they are merciless, especially with parents and teachers.

With a sly smile on their faces and mischief in their voices, they would sweetly ask, "Would you please read Bentley Beaver to us again?" Then they would look at each other and smirk, thinking I wouldn't notice. I took that as a challenge and would say yes, assuring them that *this* time I would not cry.

Going on 20 years now, I have consistently failed. I always blow it when approaching the tricky part: "On a windy day in spring, Bentley Beaver died. 'Good-bye, Bentley Beaver,'" said Belinda (his beaver wife). I'm fine until I get within a page or two of that part. Then even the anticipation of what is about to happen makes me start tearing up.

But the confusing thing is I can't figure out if I'm crying because I'm happy or because I'm sad. I suspect *The Story of Bentley Beaver* is where my tears go when I don't cry them. Bentley Beaver is my default grief-carrier, but also my joy-carrier, which suggests to me that grief and joy might spring from the same well and are inexplicably tied to each other.

Maybe that is why we can experience both at the same time. One thing is certain—when we grieve, we know it is not the end of the story. Joy is germinating within the grief, and in Christ—joy will come.

Bentley Beaver lived a long and happy life. He loved to play the guitar and sing. He had a happy marriage, happy children and happy grandchildren, so it is not a sad story. I think that is one of the reasons I cry.

Now I look back over the years and realize, by God's grace, it is the story we are also living. Any imperfections and pain are covered and redeemed by God's grace.

When Bentley grew old, he said, "I am a little scared and a little happy. Mostly I am happy, because my life has been good."

So has mine, Bentley, so has mine.

I have said these things to you, that in me you may have peace. In the world, you will have tribulations. But take heart; I have overcome the world.

—John 16:33 (ESV)

May 29, 2014

Cannon's Rainbow

When Cannon was 9-months-old, I watched him try to catch a sunbeam. Ever the keen observer, he noticed it slip through the slightly opened curtains in the den, unobtrusively, the beam thought. However, little did it realize that the minute dust particles in the air were giving it away and that it was sparkling all the way down to the floor, capturing the gaze of a curious baby boy.

Cannon smiled and crawled quickly over to the couch and pulled himself up, ready to grab the sunbeam and in all likelihood, put it in his mouth. He carefully reached out and closed his fist around the beam. Opening his hand, he studied his empty palm, turning it this way and that. Puzzled, but not one to give up easily, he decided to try again. He reached out and closed his little fingers around the beam very gently. Confidently, he quickly opened his fist to view his prize, but once again found only his empty palm. He looked back up at the sunbeam, then down again at his palm, and then cried.

Now Cannon and his twin brother, Case, are 2-years-old. A few weeks ago, they saw something ever so much bigger and better than a sunbeam—their first rainbow, and from their own backyard. How I wish I had been there. Our daughter said Case looked at it then moved on to something else, not being a rainbow kind of guy, apparently.

Cannon, however, stood at the fence and stretched his little hands up as far as he could reach, trying to touch it. When it started fading away, he cried out, "My rainbow, my rainbow." (Can it get any more poignant than that?)

The very next day, however, God surprised him with something ever so much better—a magnificent double rainbow, so big and colorful it seemed to be right in his neighborhood!

Isn't that just how it always happens? We cry and lament over what God has taken away, only to discover He had something so much bigger and more beautiful in mind than anything we could have imagined.

I like to think a rainbow is a bit of heaven breaking through for a few brief moments, giving us a glimpse of His glory. We long to capture it, but on this side of the rainbow, we cannot.

But someday, *somewhere over the rainbow*—we will, by God's grace.

I pray God will bless all four of our precious grandsons with a lifetime of sunbeams and rainbows. But even more than that, I pray for His light to make rainbows in their souls—the kind that will never fade away.

June 6, 2014

A Slowed-Down,

SERENDIPITOUS KIND OF DAY

*I*t was a slowed-down, serendipitous kind of day, unusual enough in itself but particularly so since we spent most of it in Dallas, a speeded-up city.

Byron had a PET scan scheduled at noon at one of the medical centers; it was the last screening he had to pass in order to be admitted to one of the latest Alzheimer's drug trials offered in the Dallas area. *(We found out he did qualify, and he recently received his first drug infusion.)*

After the two-hour scan, we barred the door on Alzheimer's for the day, grabbed our Jason's Deli leftovers and headed over to White Rock Lake Park. It had been a favorite place when we lived only five minutes away from it back in the '80s. I have fond memories of biking to the park and riding the lake trails with our daughter strapped into a plastic seat behind me.

We drove around the park until we found the perfect spot—a shaded picnic table on a hill covered with Indian Paintbrush and overlooking the lake. We unwrapped our leftovers and were promptly joined by a grackle (perhaps the Dallas equivalent of a seagull?), who hopped up on the table, hoping to confiscate a few crumbs. The view, sunshine and breeze bestowed a peace and tranquility that could not possibly be found even in the finest restaurant in town.

After we ate and strolled around a bit, it was time to head back to Longview. Feeling relaxed and mellow, we decided to take the "back road" (Highway 80) to Longview. It is something we almost never do because, for whatever reason, (usually grandchildren) we feel like we have to get wherever we are going in the shortest possible amount of time. I routinely set the cruise control for 5 mph over the speed limit. (I can't get a ticket for admitting that, can I?) I will blame it on our society's fast-moving, time-saving mindset.

But this was a rare "just us" day with no grandchildren.

We started tooling down the road and then realized we were not far from the most delicious peach ice cream this side of Georgia—definitely worth an impromptu side trip. So off we headed to Ham Peach Orchards in Terrell, well-known not only for its ice cream, but also for its fresh fruits and vegetables, pies, barbecue and other delectable delights.

After purchasing magnificently swirled, creamy creations in tall Styrofoam cups, we took them outside and found our second shaded picnic table of the day. (You know you are living right when you find two shady spots in one day outside of East Texas, where there is usually plenty of shade.) This spot overlooked a beautiful field and orchard, and the sunshine and breeze were still on tap.

To add to the ambiance, an Amtrak train appeared suddenly out of nowhere, roared through and then disappeared again just as quickly; its plaintive, fading wail trailing behind it. The train did not disturb but rather enhanced the peaceful atmosphere. I've always loved the sound of a train horn; my childhood was full of its reverberations.

We left Ham's with a container of fresh peaches and continued our leisurely journey down Highway 80. This time we did not mind that it meant going through every small town between Terrell and Longview. Actually it was a relief to have to go slower; I felt my stress level go down with the speedometer.

We soon shifted into "moments" gear and started noticing all sorts of common things made new at the slower speed of our minds: lots of green—the beautiful, luscious green of East Texas. You don't appreciate it until you've lived without green trees, green grass and green pastures filled with cows randomly scattered at different angles, as if placed there by a small boy. We enjoyed all manner of wildflowers and decrepit but picturesque old barns—soothing, sensory delights.

In reflection, it was a rare day of simple serendipities, made possible by slowing down and taking the back roads—not only through the towns but in our minds.

On that day, the specter of Alzheimer's disappeared like the train, leaving behind only the faintest of traces.

If I had a day that I could give you, I'd give to you a day just like today.

—John Denver

June 13, 2014

"Cover Us Up"

We were babysitting for the twins at the beginning of summer and had just put them in their cribs for the night. A few minutes later, Cannon began crying. I went back in and patted his back. He settled down, so I tiptoed back out. No dice. He started crying again, more intensely. I went back in and this time I asked him what was wrong.

It was so simple. "Cover me up," he said between sobs.

"You just want to be covered up, sweetie?" Finally being understood, he stopped crying and lay quietly holding his monkey while I covered him up. I realized it was part of a routine that made him feel loved, cared for and secure.

We all feel better when we have someone to "cover us up."

The free verse below was inspired by the "cover me up" plea, along with (if you let your imagination run free) the somewhat sinister sounds of a summer night.

The night is alive
with the pulsating cries and screams
of a thousand creatures
enshrouded in the darkness
and vocalizing en masse.

Unlike the subtle backdrop
whirring and humming
as commonly heard on
firefly-lit summer nights;
it is forceful and overbearing—
claustrophobic in its intensity.

The enigmatic darkness
savors the chaos
as it slowly encroaches,
seeking to ensnare the unaware.

"Cover us up, Father,"
the people cry
as the darkness creeps closer.
"Cloak us
with your Light."

With His mighty Light saber,
God slices through the dark
and vanquishes it,
letting loose another day—
a never-before-seen brilliant,
glorious, life-giving day.
A gift, for His people.

He will cover you with his feathers. He will shelter you with his wings. His faithful promises are your armor and protection.

—Psalm 91:4 (NLT)

July 3, 2014

The Memory Keepers

We were in the car with the dial tuned to SiriusXM mellow rock. One of my favorite songs from the '60s came on that I hadn't heard in forever—"What the World Needs Now" (by Jackie DeShannon). "Oh!" I exclaimed. "I used to sing this to our girls when they were babies."

Byron was quiet for a moment. Then he looked at me and asked, "What did I used to sing to them?"

"Why, you used to sing 'Me and My Shadow' to the girls when you rocked them to sleep," I told him.

He smiled. "I did?"

His realization of a lost cherished memory got to me more than anything has in a long time. The sadness Byron must feel when he knows he has lost precious memories of his children, his childhood, a loved one or a friend—it is heart-wrenching to think about.

I now understand more clearly the sacred trust I hold as one of the keepers of his memories.

I made a vow to myself that day to begin handing him back the gift of beloved memories more often. I want them to delight him like shooting stars in the crystallized moments that contain them before they fade away. The very nature of their rarity and fleetingness, like memories in those who live with Alzheimer's, make them a gift all the more valuable.

Now I knew what to tell our daughters to give their dad for his birthday that was coming up—their memories. They loved the idea and began compiling their lists.

The big day arrived and we all got together to celebrate. The grandsons sang "Happy Birthday" to their G-Daddy, and then we gathered in the den to watch Byron open his "memories." As he began to read them aloud, it was very hard to hold back the tears. Our daughters love their daddy so much.

Most of their memories were of ordinary days made special by the things he used to do with them as they were growing up. The ordinary things which, through time and in retrospect, have become extraordinary.

We enjoyed laughing about and reliving their various memories. Here is a sampling:

"All my friends would tell me when they saw you driving through town dressed up as Elvis, Santa, the Easter Bunny or BeeRon the clown."

"You would play 'Wake up, Little Suzie' for me in the mornings before school."

"I liked watching you in plays, especially when you were the villain."

"Seeing you work so hard at the same company and retire after so many years has shaped my work ethic in my career."

"I always had to approve your outfits before my soccer games."

"One time we were in Hastings and you were very flattered when someone mistook you for Bill Clinton."

"I liked your cooking—particularly your North Carolina barbecue and apple pies."

"You bought us a Barbie toilet that flushed."

"I always waited for you to get home from work so we could watch 'The Rockford Files' in the recliner."

"I loved playing in the tree house you built in the backyard. We had a lot of picnics up there and fun on the slide."

"We went to the Ambucs Haunted House together two years in a row, even though you thought my characters were ghoulish."

"I learned my superb ironing and clothes-folding skills from you!"

"The saying you always repeated: 'That's the *what*; now what is the *so what*?'"

When Byron finished reading, with tears in his eyes he said, "I always knew what special girls I had," then hugged his beautiful daughters.

The grandchildren played contentedly around us, oblivious to the fact that these were their precious memories in the making as well as ours.

⟶

The "*what*" is Byron has Alzheimer's.

The "*so what*" is he has a loving family

keeping his memories safeguarded in their hearts.

September 4, 2014

Epilogue

PRAYER—GOD'S SPECIAL GIFT

By Byron Horne

*E*vents of this past week—the devastation of the Gulf Coasts of Louisiana and Mississippi by Hurricane Katrina and the as yet unknown number of lives lost, and the destitute circumstances of those who have lost everything are causing many of us to seek answers from God about this tragedy.

He has given us a way to do that. It's called prayer. I think prayer is God's special gift to us. Through prayer, we can approach Him directly and personally. The prayer Jesus taught the disciples begins "Our Father who art in heaven." Just think about what that means. He who created us as His children wants to hear from us... not just our praises and thanksgivings but also our sorrows, our questions and even our frustrations.

Dorothy and I have two daughters. When they were young they had many wants and needs (sometimes those terms were interchangeable.) They made most of their requests to Dorothy because they were around her more than me—at least until I got home from work.

It was a blessing to me then when they would tell me about what they did that day, what they learned in school or what new doll or book they wanted. It's a blessing to me now when they call and ask my advice on how to handle a problem at work or how to fix something.

In the book of Genesis, we are told that God made us in His own image. I believe that He gets blessed whenever we, His children, talk to Him about our day, about our dreams, about anything at all. Now before you get the idea that everything my girls ask of me or tell me is *good* news, let me remind you that Karly is still in college and her next tuition installment is coming due soon.

God is able to take the bad news of our lives as well as the good news. He knows our hurts, our doubts, our fears and He welcomes those prayers we have that begin with the word, "Why? Why do bad things happen? Why is there war, hunger and suffering in the world?" And, "Why don't you fix it?"

Ever since creation, people have been talking to God, asking those same questions. The psalmist doesn't just praise God and rejoice in Him...he also complains, cries and pleads. Just like we do. But that's just what God wants—He wants us to bring both the good and the bad stuff to Him because He loves us. Even though there are millions of other people talking to Him at the same time, God hears each of our prayers. And he doesn't just hear...He listens. He rejoices when we rejoice and He hurts when we hurt.

In His infinite power, God listens to every single prayer coming to Him from everyone around the world. We have a God who goes one-on-one with each of us—all the time. Nobody's prayer gets put to the top of the list because we're all deserving of His attention. The Bible tells us, "The eyes of the Lord are open to the righteous, and His ears are open to their prayers" (I Peter 3:12). God doesn't have "call waiting."

Dorothy and I were careful to advise our daughters at an early age not to expect everything on their Christmas lists to appear under the tree the morning of December 25. We told them that Santa knew best what to bring and besides, our house was only so big.

We need to remember that God has that same perspective about answering our prayers: sometimes the answer is "Yes," sometimes it is "No," sometimes it's "Later" and sometimes it's "Trust Me." Trust—now, that's hard for me to do.

I tend to think I can handle things myself and thank God later for being there to come to the rescue in case those things don't work out. Yeah, control, that's what it's all about. With an attitude like that, in God's classroom I do a lot of learning the same lesson over and over.

I began my career with the Texas Employment Commission in January of 1976. A year later, I married Dorothy and after a couple of apartments, we bought a house near White Rock Lake in Dallas. Things were going well at work. I liked my job, the promotions were coming, and I got good performance reviews. I had control over things. I went to the office, did my job, worked hard and had a great future.

A couple of years later, I found out how little control I had over that future. It was at that time the State of Texas experienced a big financial crisis and all state agencies were told to do more with less. Budgets were being slashed and the only way to continue to operate was to reduce staff. The decision was made to base the layoffs on seniority. My job going away became more than a possibility and I had no control over that. All the hard work and positive perfor-mance reviews couldn't stop a layoff.

God answered my prayers with, "Trust Me." It wasn't easy for me to do that—giving control to Him. I prayed that His will would be done and that I would be obedient to that will. I trusted Him. January 10, 2006, will be my 30th year with the Texas Workforce Commission. To God be the Glory.

Scripture tells us in I Corinthians 13:12, "Now we see through a glass darkly but soon face to face." God gave us prayer so that we can get a little preview of what it's like to be in His presence, talking with Him and listening to Him tell us He loves us.

Today we share our joy, our pain, and our needs with Him through the dark glass of faith. But we know that one day we will see Him face to face.

And prayer will become reunion.

2005

ABOVE: MARK, AMANDA, NATHANIEL AND KARL

BELOW: TREY, KARLY, CASE AND CANNON

G-DADDY AND DOT-DOT WITH CASE, KARL, NATHANIEL AND CANNON

About Dorothy and Byron

Dorothy and Byron had an unlikely but fortuitous meeting on a blind date in 1974 while he was stationed in Fort Hood, Texas, and she was a college student in Monroe, Louisiana. He was a man of faith and also a singer, songwriter, musician, artist and the funniest person she had ever met (except for maybe his puns). She (mostly) got used to them, though, because they have now been married for 38 years. Their greatest joys are their two daughters and sons-in-law and four precious grandsons along with Angus, their schnauzer. They are also blessed with a wonderful church family and great friends.

Byron worked for the state of Texas for 30 years and as a side-line, entertained and delighted hundreds of children and adults over the years with his various personae: BeeRon the Clown, Elvis, Santa Claus and the Easter Bunny, to name a few. Back in the late '80s and early '90s, he also acted in many of the Longview Community Theatre plays. Nowadays, Byron loves acting silly with his grandsons, having coffee with friends, playing guitar as part of the church worship team, being a member of the marvelous Unforgettable Tuesdays day club and watching old TV shows and movies.

Dorothy (who sounds really boring compared to Byron) taught first (mostly) and second grades for 20 years and still misses her now-grownup "children." These days she likes to sit in the backyard under the mulberry tree and read or write. When she is not doing that, she likes walking on nature trails and taking pictures of ordinary glories. Her secret passion is playing bongo drums.

Trust in the Lord with all your heart,
And do not lean on your own understanding.
In all your ways acknowledge Him,
And He will make straight your paths.

—Proverbs 3:5, 6 (ESV)

Made in the USA
San Bernardino, CA
27 November 2017